The BARN

AN EXTRAORDINARY TRUE STORY

BY DAVID HILL

The Barn: An Extraordinary True Story

Trilogy Christian Publishers
A Wholly Owned Subsidiary of Trinity Broadcasting Network
2442 Michelle Drive, Tustin, CA 92780

Rights Department, 2442 Michelle Drive, Tustin, CA 92780.

Trilogy Christian Publishing/TBN and colophon are trademarks of Trinity Broadcasting Network.

For information about special discounts for bulk purchases, please contact Trilogy Christian Publishing.

Cover design by Elisha Bennett Coad

Manufactured in the United States of America
10 9 8 7 6 5 4 3 2 1
Library of Congress Cataloging in Publication Data is available.

ISBN: 978-1-68556-647-0
E-ISBN: 978-1-68556-648-7

To my four beloved sons:
Solomon, Gabriel, Isaiah, and Seth.

May God bless my imperfect reflection
of our Heavenly Father's love to help you navigate
safe passage into a rich spiritual inheritance.

Acknowledgments

To Jules, my sparkling jewel, my beautiful wife and faithful companion for life. Thank you for working alongside me on this three-year endeavor. Partnering with you, searching to find the best writer within me, proved invaluable. May we enjoy the fruit of our labor.

To my God-fearing mother, Susan, from whom I received my spiritual inheritance. Thank you for crying out in tireless intercession for me, which moved the heart of God. Your prayers helped save me and provided the foundation for this testimony of God's grace and glory.

To my beloved brother in blood and Spirit and best friend, Roy. Thank you for providing the inspiration for this book title and helping maintain a historically accurate narrative. The torturous beginnings that we endured together created a powerful lifetime bond and a special place in my heart for you, Roy d'Boy. I look forward to exploring the infinite vastness and glorious wonders of Heaven with you for all eternity.

To Carolin Bennett Coad, my chief editor extraordinaire and dear friend, it was a privilege observing a discerning literary sculptor extracting a diamond in the rough. Your commitment to this arduous task demonstrated exceptional patience and diligence. Most endearing was your prayerful approach before and devotion during each editing session. I will forever be thankful.

To the initially unknown coeditor, surprisingly announced to me as we neared the end of the editing process: Jimmy DeMet, 88 years young and an elite athlete who has competed in over 300 triathlons, 50 marathons including 4 Boston Marathons, and a World Games Hall of Famer. Thank you for sacrificing over three and a half years of your life in sharing your insight, along with your prayerful devotion.

To distinguished author Frank Peretti, I offer my appreciation for giving your valuable time to read my manuscript. Your affirmation, as expressed through your deeply touching and personal response, was exceptionally rewarding to me as a writer.

And foremost, to my incomprehensibly awesome, loving Heavenly Father. I am most thankful to You for giving me the desire to share this true story with the rest of the world. I dedicate this book for Your glory.

Contents

Preface

For many years, I have wrestled with a relentless stirring to write this book. Finally, tossing procrastination aside, I gave way to this daunting task, which posed several important considerations. Foremost among my concerns was placing my credibility at risk for describing scarcely believable extraordinary supernatural events. Also, it is humbling to recount my past personal life and share intimate and unflattering details.

Regardless, there is a higher purpose to which I remain loyal and unapologetically steadfast. This purpose is to provide a bird's-eye view of how my perilous journey began and how it led me to an unexpected destination. As this incredible yet true story unfolds, I am hopeful you will discover this book to be captivating, compelling, and inspirational.

CHAPTER 1

Dire Beginnings

"**N**o thanks, I think I'll pass." That would have been my response when my ticket came up to enter the world. If requesting a change of venue with better circumstances wasn't granted, I would have pleaded to never venture forth. As I recount how my story unfolds, you will understand why.

At age four, my highly inquisitive nature nearly cost me my life several times. It all began at my grandmother Margaret's home in Minnesota. One of my aunts drove up and parked her white Ford Falcon in front of my grandmother's hillside home. After my aunt entered the house, I decided to take her car for a quick spin, thinking I could return before anyone noticed. Behind the car and across a sloping driveway about a hundred feet away was a steep river embankment. I left the car door open just in case my plan went awry. Grabbing the steering column shifter with both hands, I yanked it down with all my might. As the car started rolling backward, I noticed that the brakes didn't seem to work as I stood on the brake pedal with both feet. Suddenly, I realized that my little trip wasn't going as planned; and I bailed out of the driver's seat. I fell out flat on my belly. The front tire narrowly missed my head, running over my right hand. I jumped up to watch the car quickly roll backward as it gained speed down the driveway before heading for the steep river embankment. Thankfully, the car veered off toward a large roll of wire fencing propped up against a corner post, bouncing off of it like a spring before coming to a final stop. Turning around, I saw my mother, grandmother, and aunt standing outside with mouths gaping wide open, frozen in stunned amazement. I should have received the worst spanking ever. Instead, I felt as though I was suffocated from a flood of incoming hugs for escaping a near-death experience. An abundant supply of sympathy was administered before any first aid for an injured right hand that would bear permanent scarring. And, I would always be able to share this outlandish tale about surviving a car accident with the car ending up without even a scratch.

That same summer, my mother sternly warned me not to go up the hill across the driveway from our mobile home. On the hillside, there was a large ground nest of hornets, which I was supposed to stay far away from. I asked my mother where it was so I would be certain not to "accidentally" go anywhere near the area. From a safe distance, she pointed to the general vicinity where the nest was located. Yet it wasn't long before I found a stick and began walking up the hillside in search of the hornets' nest. My world of wonder suddenly turned into a nightmare as I discovered that poking the nest with a stick was not a good idea. I was immediately swarmed by a thick cloud of hornets. Screaming in panic and in excruciating pain, my mother heard my wailing and came rushing out of the house. She ran up the hill, swooped me up, and somehow began stripping off my clothes on the run back down the hill heading toward the house. As the deep humming buzz of hornets continued to swarm all around, I was stung inside my ears, mouth, eyelids, under my clothes, and even on certain areas considered to be private. Hearing the commotion, my father and uncles came running from my grandparents' nearby barnyard to help, and I found myself suddenly being tossed into a bathtub of water. Bedridden for several days and miraculously dodging anaphylactic shock from hundreds of stings, I quickly turned to other areas of childhood research and never again poked a hornets' nest.

The following winter, I was at my grandmother Margaret's house on a bitterly cold sunny morning. A storm had just rolled through the night before, dumping several feet of fresh snow. I eagerly bundled up to go outside. Awaiting me was our large family dog, Rowdy. He had a thick tuft of light brown hair encircling his neck that gave him the look of a lion. I usually followed Rowdy around wherever he went, and this bright winter morning was no exception. I wanted to go on an expedition that would take me farther than I ever had gone before. As I looked into Rowdy's eager eyes, he seemed to know that, too. Off we went, trudging together through the soft, fluffy snow with my companion leading the way. It seemed like a long time had passed before I turned around and noticed that the farmplace was just a speck in the distance, and then it disappeared behind a grove of trees about a half-mile away. By now, Rowdy was well ahead of me and had come to the embankment of a frozen river. Looking ahead, I saw there was an unexplored forest on the other side. The mystery of uncharted territory called me, and any concern of safe passage was ignored. With

Rowdy still leading the way into the wooded unknown, I was drawn to continue our adventure.

Halfway across the river, I suddenly fell through the ice and found myself desperately splashing around in deep freezing water, grasping for any shelf of ice thick enough to support my weight. After a long struggle, I was somehow able to climb out of the water, my snowsuit soon frozen stiff like thick cardboard. Even so, I still wanted to search for another route across the frozen river to catch up with Rowdy, wherever he had gone. Eventually I decided to return home without him and began my journey back. It wasn't long before I heard the distant shouts of my father and uncle, who had been tracking me. Aware that I was at risk of freezing to death, they suddenly picked me up and began tossing me back and forth like a football between each other to lighten the load as they trudged through the deep snow as quickly as possible. Back at my grandmother Margaret's house, I found myself once again being stripped down and tossed into a tub of warm water. Miraculously, I did not drown that day or die of hypothermia. And thankfully, Rowdy turned up to lick my face later.

My twenty-four-year-old father and mother and my brother, Roy, and I lived on a small dairy farm in a mobile home next to a steep river embankment. The farm was where my grandmother Margaret lived and where my father was born and raised. Our homestead could be found in a seemingly endless winding river valley that was surrounded by lush soybean fields and cornfields, which dressed the region with a colorful patchwork of vibrant greens and yellows. Foothills arose and dotted the landscape, overshadowing the river valley with their thick canopies of century-old elm and oak trees, providing many pleasant vistas. Within this uniquely pictur-esque region, my home was nestled less than a mile outside the farming community of Winnebago's 1,700 residents in southern Minnesota.

Growing up as a brown-haired, blue-eyed farm boy, I was athletic and loved to play hard. It was natural to be filthy and soaked in sweat. If my grass-stained blue jeans could have spoken, they would've protested their reckless owner having holes or patches on the knees. Sports was my passion, espe-cially playing football. I found great delight in watching the Minnesota Vikings dominate their division in the NFL with Fran "The Man" Tarkenton as quarterback leading the way.

My mother told me that I was a good boy with a sensitive heart. She said that I was physically gifted and intelligent. My mother also believed that I had a talent for singing. She must have been right because when I sang, everyone listened. Upon my family's request, it was a tradition that I round up a trio to sing Christmas carols at my grandma Pearl's house. My trio always included my two-year younger, blonde-haired, blue-eyed brother, Roy d'Boy, a little guy for his age with a small Pillsbury Doughboy belly, and my younger cousin. A large group of relatives, including grandparents, aunts, uncles, and cousins, gathered around to listen. Afterward, Roy, my cousin, and I were rewarded with rousing applause.

Despite my mother's favorable impressions of me, I battled the emotional trauma of my parents' combative relationship. Before my mother and father's painful divorce, a searing memory was etched into my childhood of one of their violent fights. One day when I was five years old, I was sitting along-side my little brother, Roy, on the couch. We watched our mother screaming as she tried to shield herself from our father. He was straddled on top of her, striking endless blows to her head. I could not take it any longer. Fearing that my mother would not survive the assault, I dared to run over and jump on my father's back, only to find myself looking up at the ceiling after he effortlessly shook me off.

My father grew up in a dysfunctional setting. His father, Ira, was a dairy farmer. Ira was also the local milkman, and his lifestyle bore the negative connotations associated with the title. My grandfather was a prolific seed sower who had left behind a first wife with six daughters in North Dakota before marrying my grandmother and raising a second large family. A book was later written in 1992 by one of my grandfather's daughters from his first marriage entitled *The Depression of The Dirty Thirties*.[1] As my aunt penned her experience, she described how it was the last straw for her mother when Ira tried to bring home a pregnant woman to live under their roof.

My grandfather, Ira, also possessed a volatile disposition. During the last year of his life when I was only five, I remember him wheelchair-bound with a plaid wool blanket draped over his frail lap. There didn't seem to be much wrong with my grandfather's lungs, however. He often pierced the air with the sound of loud, sharp profanities laced with God's name yelled in vain as he called down curses upon his children. Because of Ira's violent temper, the decrepit old man scared me.

My father was born in the middle of eight siblings. His bigger size was an anomaly amongst them. He was also the rowdiest and most rebellious of them all. Stories about my father's upbringing were so outlandish that they grew to folktale status. My grandmother, Margaret, whom I was fond of, had a kinder, gentler side. Nevertheless, she must have been tested on many occasions in her unruly family. One well-known story was when my grandmother took a roasting chicken out of the oven only to discover it had already been ripped apart by her children like a pack of hungry wolves. If any thieving children were caught in the act, they ran for their lives, stuffing their mouths on the run down the long driveway while being chased by other hungry and angry siblings yelling death threats.

One time my father's youngest brother was being beaten by his oldest sister. In an effort to save his brother, my father snuck up behind her and punched her between the eyes. As the two brothers ran out the door to escape, their sister hurled a large meat cleaver at them. Thankfully, it fell short of its intended target and split the door with half of its heavy, massive blade protruding out the other side.

Another well-known story originated from a neighboring property owner named Pete. One day he set out a bucketful of scraps left over from the supper table for his dog. Pete warned him that if he ate all of it, he was going to shoot him in the head. Sure enough, being a dog, he ate all of the table scraps. And, true to his word, Pete shot him in the head. The word quickly spread. From then on, if my grandfather, Ira, found any of his boys eating too much, he warned them that he would take them over to Pete's. This story was passed down to the next generation. As a teenager, I was warned on numerous occasions by my father and uncles that my voracious appetite could earn me a trip to Pete's.

Two of my father's brothers chose acceptable ways to channel their excessive energy. Both of them were accomplished in wrestling and track and finished high school. Local car racing at the track was big back then, and both brothers raced. One drove a modified '62 Corvette and the other a '63 Ford Falcon, both winning their share of races. However, my father, along with two older brothers, dropped out of school. By the time my father was a freshman dropout, his notorious reputation was well established for illegal drag racing, having engaged in several high-speed hot pursuits with the law. It wasn't long before my father's triple carburetor '54 Ford took him on a speedy trip to jail with his license finally being revoked.

In stark contrast to my father's homelife, my mother was raised in a more gentle-dispositioned family. They owned a several thousand-acre crop farm. She was the second of five siblings with an older and younger brother and two much younger sisters. In every way, my mother was a beautiful woman with her dark curly hair and sparkling brown eyes. Her radiant smile and joyful personality could brighten anyone's day. Her father, Ellsworth, was beloved throughout the community of Winnebago, Minnesota, and was nicknamed "Hap" for his happy disposition. In addition to farming the land with his two sons, my grandfather owned Lucky Lanes, the local bowling alley, that was always hopping as the most popular place in town. If there was anyone more beloved than Hap, it was my grandmother, Pearl, who personified a pure gem. Her joyful and loving soul, along with her delectable and copious cooking, was the magnet that attracted our large extended family to gather for all types of occasions. I could never imagine having greater grandparents than Hap and Pearl.

My mother, however, was the black sheep of the family. Decisions she made while growing up were not always in keeping with the best wishes of her parents. Unlike her family, who was calculating and committed to long-term goals, my mother was carefree and spontaneous. Her discretion was passionately overridden to draw the most out of every moment. She threw caution to the wind making choices with inherent risks. My mother was fifteen when she saw my father for the first time. Even having his fast car impounded for reckless driving didn't seem to slow down his ability to get around. My father rode bareback shirtless and barefoot with hands full of mane, hoofs kicking up clods of black earth high into the air as he galloped across one of her family's plowed fields hooting and hollering the whole way. The alluring sight quickly drew my mother into a relationship with him that would supposedly free her from the boredom of her family's sensibilities. My parents married three years later when they both turned eighteen.

As my father entered his mid-twenties, he was considered by some to be a man's man. He stood six feet one on a broad-shouldered hefty frame that carried two hundred and forty pounds. With his thick full beard, he looked like a lumberjack. My father's sandy blonde hair, blue eyes, and rugged good looks were the bait that he used to reel in the many women willing to stand in line. His insatiable sexual appetite drove him away from our family, but not before he had an affair with an older brother's wife. My father's dalliance with her resulted in a pregnancy, causing his brother's marriage to end in divorce. Embittered, his brother became estranged from the rest of the family. My father also impregnated an eighteen-year-old girl. They were engaged to be married before my parents were even divorced. Even though my father's sexual promiscuity was destructive, he was unabashedly proud and flaunted his licentiousness. He printed out a sentence in all caps with raised white letters on a black plastic adhesive label, "I AM THE HORNY BULL." He stuck the label to the dashboard of his '64 three-quarter-ton Chevy truck with a powerful engine and six-inch lift kit. There, his declaration remained for many years. Mystery clouded my understanding of the label's meaning until I grew older and had lived through the pain of its implications.

Growing up, I wrestled over which scenario I would have chosen. Might it have been better to have been fatherless or to have a father such as mine who was unfaithful to my mother and beat her in front of Roy and me? Would I have chosen to have been fatherless or have had one like mine who was like a tornado that quickly blew through, uprooting and ripping apart our lives and leaving us behind? It wasn't until later as a young adult that I began to heal from the inner turmoil associated with my father's abandonment.

The burdens following my parents' divorce fell upon my abandoned single mother. Needing to pack up and relocate, she rented a small house situated along one of the few streets of the unincorporated town of nearby Huntley, Minnesota. During that time, I recall sitting alone with a sharp pain burning in my soul. Not knowing how to deal with that kind of pain, I tried to yell it out. When that didn't work, I wanted to kill myself, ultimately believing there was no hope of ever escaping a cruel world void of peace and happiness. However, as a five-year-old, not even my inquisitive nature could lure me into the dark unknown to discover what it would be like to choke to death while dangling at the end of a rope.

One summer morning, I stood in the living room looking at my mother lying on the couch. Perpetually heartbroken and sickened with distress, she cried most of the time. Again, a steady stream of tears flowed down my mother's cheeks. This time, however, seemed to be worse when I noticed white pills scattered around the room. And then one of her arms fell limp to the floor. Thankfully, a kind and gracious older neighbor lady whom I fondly remember named Greta was keenly aware that our broken family was hurting and kept us on her caring heart. Greta's concern prompted her to regularly stop by to check up on us. On this particular morning, she discovered my mother collapsed on the couch, fading into a state of lifelessness. It was then I knew that something was desperately wrong when Greta screamed after several unsuccessful attempts to wake up my mother.

During that anxious time, not knowing if my mother was going to live or die, Roy and I were placed in the care of our grandparents, Hap and Pearl, whose farm was nearby. Several weeks later, my mother recovered and was released from the hospital. Roy and I were reunited with her and returned home. Despite the unfortunate circumstances that continued to hold her captive, she fought to keep herself together. Even so, I never for one moment doubted my mother's love for us.

In 1971, when I was eight, my mother began taking Roy and me to church regularly. During this time, my life was transformed by the profound influence of our pastor, Reverend Stimpson. He was a godly man who honorably served our community by providing much-needed moral leadership. Without a consistent male role model in my life, our pastor's loving and kind influence tempered my anger and confusion and etched a positive indelible imprint upon my soul. As my mother, Roy, and I continued attending his church, a desire was planted in my heart. I wanted to unreservedly commit my life to Christ and become a minister of the Gospel someday just like Reverend Stimpson. My desire confirmed a prophetic declaration made by my mother the day I was born. God had impressed upon her heart that I was called to be a minister of the Gospel.

Deeply influenced by God's lovingkindness, I wanted to shout to the rest of the world that I had fallen in love with God. This desire compelled me to publicly confess my faith through water baptism. However, I needed to persuade my mother and Reverend Stimpson to be the first eight-year-old in the church's history granted this exception. The policy for attending the adult-oriented baptism class needed to be changed. Since my mother and Reverend Stimpson sensed my resolve to be baptized would be difficult to suppress, they determined it wise to honor my request. Nevertheless, it was made clear that I would have to complete the class while demonstrating that I understood the symbolic meaning of water baptism.

It was a special, sunny Sunday morning baptismal service when I expressed before a congregation of several hundred people that I had received God's love and forgiveness in my heart. Coming up out of that baptismal, I felt pure and fresh. Like Samuel in the Old Testament, when God called him as a young boy, I also innocently and enthusiastically responded to His call, "Here I am…Speak, for your servant is listening" (1 Samuel 3:4b, 10b).

Later that year, our mother made a terrible decision which subjected Roy and me to an inescapable and fateful journey.

In an attempt to rebound from the rejection of her first love, she began a desperate search to replace a missing in action husband and father. My mother started dating a local farmer. Upon being introduced to him, I felt very uncomfortable as I detected a meanness lurking inside this cold stranger. My apprehension would later turn into full-blown fear.

This new man was ten years older than my mother and stood five feet nine on a floppy frame of two hundred and fifty pounds. Even though he wore baggy blue jeans, they were unable to contain his protruding potbelly that drooped over his waistline while exposing an unsightly condition of severe plumber's crack on his backside. His tight, yellow armpit-stained T-shirt revealed ghostly pale, flabby arms and the outline of a sagging chest. His T-shirt was typically stained with brown streaks of Copenhagen juice which streamed down from the corners of his mouth onto his collar and chest. His speech was muffled with a mouth perpetually stuffed with snuff. If he were to ever smile, it would reveal a thick black tarlike substance that stuck to his upper and lower gumlines. The few long thin strands of light-colored hair on his balding head blew around loosely in the wind, giving him an unkempt institutionalized look.

All throughout their dating relationship, I had desperately hoped that the whole thing would just simply come to an end. As beautiful as my mother was, I daydreamed about her finding another man like Glen Campbell, believing that she could effortlessly captivate any man with her beauty and charm. It wasn't long, however, before my mother asked Roy and me how we felt about this man becoming our stepfather. The idea frightened me. I vehemently pleaded with my mother not to marry him, expressing that I did not like anything about this man and thought he was mean as well as repulsive in appearance.

I felt threatened, so I had desperately hoped that our mother's love for Roy and me would awaken her to see what I saw in this man and compel her to protect us. However, her desperation overrode her maternal instincts. Sadly, my mother fell prey to the fateful decision to marry him. Driven by our dislike for this new stepfather, Roy and I would never call him Dad. Only on rare occasions when necessity dictated would we awkwardly refer to him by his name, Dale. Living with him would become a fateful six-year hellish nightmare. Irrevocable circumstances bringing a whirlwind of unspeakable trauma and suffering were now set into motion. Sentenced to the darkest time in our lives, how we survived our torment will forever remain a miraculous mystery to my mother, Roy, and me.

CHAPTER 2

Genesis of a Diabolical Plan

Because I turned my life over to God and every fiber of my being ached to please Him, a spiritual bull's-eye was placed on my back. It felt like an evil force was scheming to terminate my newfound relationship with God. A violent dark storm was dispatched and quickly approached from just over the hill and around the next blind corner.

Not long after moving to Dale's farm, my mother, Roy, and I helped load his pickup truck and camper, destined for a fishing trip to Rapid City, South Dakota, for our first and final family vacation. Within four hours' driving time, we experienced a flat tire. Popping open a storage compartment that housed the lug wrench and jack, Dale noticed that a fishing rod was tangled up. Unsuccessful in quickly untangling the line, he became enraged and began shouting, swearing, and blaming Roy and me for the mess. After throwing the fishing rod back inside the compartment and changing the tire, Dale hopped into the cab with gritted teeth, turning the truck around to return to the farm without saying a word. As my mother attempted to change his mind, I feared that she might easily push him to the brink, thereby risking his wrath. Thankfully, her instinct prompted her to remain silent before it was too late. Returning to Dale's farm, I was devastated. Our family vacation thwarted, I realized that it would not have been enjoyable anyway with a man with whom I already felt unsafe.

After returning to Dale's farm, Roy's and my safety was unknowingly placed at great risk. One day, I noticed a wooden box in his garage with rope handles that was staged next to a stand-alone metal grinder and arc welder. The old box looked as though it had been long forgotten and had sat there for many years. It was greasy and grimy, with something wet seeping through. There were deep black scorch marks on the wooden lid caused by sparks generated from the nearby grinder and welder. With Roy at my side, I removed the top of the box. I was surprised to discover explosives that reminded me of a scene from a *Road Runner* cartoon, courtesy of the ACME Corporation. Inside were two dozen soggy, unstable sticks of dynamite. Roy had been a superintendent of the world's largest road construction company with a Master Blaster license. In retrospect, he wondered how we were not blown to smithereens playing around with unstable dynamite stored near hazardous heat sources.

One fall Friday evening, we all loaded up in my mother's 1968 Olds destined for town to watch a Winnebago High School homecoming football game. Just as we pulled onto the highway, there was a loud ear-piercing explosion inside the vehicle. Suddenly, the interior of the car was showered with shattered glass. A large buck had leaped through the driver's side rear window where Roy was seated. Frantically searching to escape, the animal began kicking and thrashing wildly.

An intense moment later, the buck escaped after ramming the other passenger side rear window next to me, shattering the glass. My mother climbed into the back seat to assess the severity of the bloody cuts and bruises Roy had sustained. While attending to him, she was shocked to discover that I was miraculously unscathed. Overruling my mother's vehement urging to take Roy to the hospital, Dale belligerently turned the car around and returned to the farm. While cleaning up my brother's head injuries, my mother discovered numerous small shards of glass embedded in his skull. She tediously tried to extract each one. However, later Roy felt a large piece of glass still stuck so deeply in his head that it was not visible and therefore overlooked by our mother. As he wiggled and twisted the shard, Roy could hear the sound of the glass moving inside his head. So he grabbed ahold of the two-inch-long by one-inch-wide chunk and yanked it out. My mother returned to check on Roy only to discover blood gushing from his head and coming out of both of his ears.

Nearly forty years later in 2009, Roy received a CT brain scan which revealed a two-inch deep scar in his brain along with previous signs of blood clotting. This examination drew the immediate attention of several doctors, including a highly regarded brain surgeon brought down from another floor. He knew of no safe surgical procedure to remove the glass without causing a permanent vegetative state or killing the patient. Curiosity prompted the surgeon to ask Roy for the name of the doctor whom he presumed had extracted the shard. The brain surgeon was astonished to discover that Roy had wiggled and twisted the glass shard to yank it out. The doctor informed my brother that he should have died instantly or ended up in a permanent vegetative state when the glass initially penetrated his brain. He was so amazed by Roy's extraordinary story that he acknowledged it was a miracle. The brain surgeon requested permission to use Roy's CT scan to share with his colleagues in seminars that he conducted across the country.

Within a year of Dale's marriage to my mother, he sold his Winnebago, Minnesota, farm to my grandfather, Hap, and two uncles. Our family then moved to another farm that Dale purchased two hundred miles upstate in the remote woodlands of northern Minnesota twenty miles northwest of the nearest small town of Hinckley. His decision to promptly walk away from a multigenerational million-dollar crop farm that yielded impressive profits year after year seemed baffling and indefensible.

In contrast, the next farm Dale purchased was the ugliest eyesore anyone could imagine. A circular driveway took its course in front of an old, dilapidated dairy barn situated in the middle of the farm. Because the barn's lean was so extreme from front to back, I felt anxious entering it and would have preferred taking the risk of walking into an old condemned mineshaft. Inside the barn there were rickety timbers straining to support the sagging ceiling and a hayloft loaded with tons of moldy hay. The barn was also infested with rats and flies. Several calf stalls appeared to have never been cleaned and contained maggot-infested manure up to three feet deep. Throughout the entire barn, various types of mold seemed to display more colors than the rainbow. All the other outbuildings consisted of old, rusty tin sheds with the exception of a rotted wooden granary and corn crib and both sat on crumbling cement foundations.

The modest 1950s house came with an unfinished upstairs and dank unfinished cellar. Next to the house was a small detached garage. On the other side of the garage was an unsightly, deep winding ravine infested with nettle weeds five to six feet high. The ravine encroached the building site like an ugly snake that had slithered up from a stagnant swamp down below. Even worse, the ravine was used as a garbage dump where all sorts of debris had been haphazardly tossed for what appeared to be decades. The dump was filled with tires, mattresses, bedsprings and frames, and rusted burn barrels. Two adjacent feedlots behind the barn appeared to have never been cleaned. Each contained multiple mountain-sized piles of moldy cow manure and ponds of liquid muck a foot deep. Fencing throughout the 400-acre farm was in disrepair, with complete sections missing. Half of the farmland consisted of overused rocky pasture ground, while the remaining land was designated for hayfields.

After walking through the barn and outbuildings, I simply wanted to run away and hide. A sinking feeling of doom came over me as I realized that I had no choice but to call this ugly eyesore my home. Looking back, I now realize that Dale's reasoning behind such a move was clearly driven by malicious intent. Framed in a spiritual context, he seemed to be possessed by some unknown dark force to purchase this remote rundown farm. Isolation was the first step in Dale's evil plan. It would shut off contact with my mother's family and prevent anyone knowing the terrible things to which my mother, Roy, and I would soon be subjected. "Be alert and of sober mind. Your enemy the devil prowls around like a roaring lion looking for someone to devour" (1 Peter 5:8).

Incredibly, during the course of the next six years, Roy and I helped Dale develop a viable farming operation. The workload forced upon us required the strength and stamina of an adult. We were harnessed to long hours of physically strenuous labor like yearling oxen. My mother regarded Dale's work demands as grossly inappropriate for boys our age. As the fear of Dale intensified, she was unable to address this issue. Furthermore, three half-brothers were born, which created a significant complication for her to challenge Dale. Therefore, divorce was no longer a feasible option for my mother. Raising five children on her own would be far more difficult than it had been raising just two. In addition, her parents would undoubtedly characterize a divorce as another one of my mother's poor choices.

Roy and I helped Dale milk twenty-five dairy cows twice a day. We accomplished this task the old-fashioned way by using handheld milking machines, buckets, and milk cans. Stall and gutter cleaning was performed morning and evening with a single tire wheelbarrow. There were twenty or more loads to shovel, haul, and dump per cleaning. Each load of heavy sloshing manure had to be carefully balanced while being wheeled down a steep wooden ramp into the deep muck. The greatest challenge was wheeling the load a considerable distance over to a large mountain of manure. There were one hundred head of Angus beef cattle that Roy and I grain-fed twice daily. Numerous trips were made for each graining, which entailed dragging two five-gallon buckets from the granary to the feedlot. Trying to get through the deep sticky muck, many times one or even both of my rubber boots took on a mind of their own. They broke ranks and refused to follow, leaving me stranded in my socks.

Every summer from the ages of eight to fourteen, Roy and I stood side by side on a hay trailer. It was hitched behind a square baler that Dale pulled with his 706 International tractor. Using hooks, we took turns pulling the bales off the rear chute and stacking them. The trailer was loaded with up to one hundred and fifty bales, each weighing fifty to seventy-five pounds, and was stacked six to eight bales high. Even though Roy and I worked as fast as we could, there were times, especially when younger, we were unable to keep up with the fast pace of bales spitting out the rear chute. As unstacked bales began to pile up on the front of the trailer, they fell off onto the ground. Rather than slow down or momentarily stop the tractor so Roy and I could catch up, Dale would jump off and run back to slap Roy and me alongside the head.

One particular day, Roy and I had extra help baling hay as my mother drove the tractor, pulling the baler and hay trailer. Roy's job was to hook the bales coming out of the chute. Dale stood behind him, grabbed the bales, and carried them over to the rear of the thirty-foot-long trailer. From there, Dale threw the bales up to me; and I stacked them. The metal hay hooks had six-inch-long, sharp-tipped shanks, which looked like a replacement for a pirate's missing hand. As Roy let his hay hook fly to snag the next bale, it ricocheted off. Suddenly, the shank penetrated below his right kneecap. Incapacitated and preoccupied with the hook lodged in his leg, the bales quickly piled up. Dale was angry and came racing over to see what was causing the holdup. Roy saw Dale look in my direction and then my mother's to see that our backs were turned. Dale then grabbed the nearest bale and intentionally swung it around, body slamming my brother with such force that it caused him to sail off the hay trailer. Roy ended up landing on his knees. Upon impact, the entire curved hook penetrated under his kneecap. I turned around and saw Roy lying on the ground. Then I looked at Dale, who kept on moving bales, acting as if he was oblivious to what had just happened. I yelled at my mother to stop the tractor. As she and I approached Roy, he had already yanked the hook out of his blood-soaked knee and was sitting in a puddle of blood. I wanted to help them on their long walk back to the house, but Dale told me to stay behind. He ordered my mother and Roy to return and continue our grueling labor after she had treated my brother's wound.

A 3 or 4 hay crop cutting season produced 10,000 bales per year. Roy and I worked ten to twelve hours each day baling in breezeless humid conditions under a blistering ninety to one-hundred-degrees summer sun. After the hay trailers were full, they were transported into a large tin shed. There the trailers were unloaded, and we restacked the hay fifteen to twenty bales high. Working inside the shed was even more unbearable, as it amplified the heat like a Dutch oven.

In addition to our extremely long workdays baling hay, our daily chores included barn cleaning and feeding and watering the cattle, chickens, and pigs. These additional responsibilities added one to two hours of work each morning and evening for Roy and me. During the school year, we did our chores before and after school. With a one-hour bus ride to school and back, it was not uncommon for us to put in a twelve-hour day, including school during the week, before we could finally eat supper and go to bed. On weekends, Roy and I worked fourteen to sixteen hours a day. Going to bed each night, we were exhausted, carrying a heavy load of physical and psychological stress.

The days Roy and I didn't bale hay, we were sent out to the pasture to handpick rocks using a hay trailer hitched to an old John Deere tractor. After loading the trailer with rocks, I drove the tractor pulling the loaded trailer to dumpsites where they were offloaded. Roy and I also helped repair and install miles of wooden post barbed wire fence. We dug up to twenty-five postholes each day on fence building jobs using shovels and a handheld posthole digger. One time when Roy and I were building a fence, I lost a claw hammer. After searching for hours, I had to report the lost tool to Dale. He was furious and about to make me pedal my bike twenty miles to town and back to purchase a new hammer. Thankfully, my mother boldly stepped in to intervene, prayerfully helping me find the tool I had lost.

My mother was also overworked. Not only did she help with the farm responsibilities, but she also performed all household duties, tended a large garden, and took care of my three younger half-brothers. Despite all that my mother did, she was still somehow able to lay out a hardy breakfast; a huge lunch, which was the same as a dinner for most; and an evening spread fit for a king, all made completely from scratch.

No matter how hard Roy and I worked, it was never enough to satisfy Dale. Too many self-imposed demands and deadlines created a highly stressful environment. This further destabilized Dale's impatient disposition and volatile temper. He would spiral further out of control. His yelling and name-calling, followed by slaps to the face or cuffs alongside the head, became more frequent. Psychological games and traps were introduced and used to set the stage for Dale's even more intense hostile actions.

Typically, Dale would hop on the tractor and head down our two-hundred-foot driveway, deliberately traveling a considerable distance with the engine revved up, his mouth stuffed full of Copenhagen, before blurting out a muffled command that was impossible to decipher. When he returned and saw Roy and me standing befuddled and frozen in fear, this ignited his temper, causing him to explode in an uncontrollable fit of rage. Dale would jump off the tractor, sometimes before coming to a stop, and storm toward us. With gritted teeth and tobacco juice spewing out of his cussing mouth, I didn't have to guess what was in store for Roy and me. The only thing we could do was cower and try to shield our heads while screaming out, "Sorry, sorry!", knowing we were about to receive a severe beating. Strategically without leaving a mark, Dale would repeatedly slap us off balance between his manure-encrusted gloves. Roy and I suffered a deafening ringing in our ears, seeing sparks as we were beaten and sometimes even left lying on the ground unconscious.

As the beatings occurred with increasing intensity and regularity, Roy and I brainstormed a plan, hoping to avoid the next assault. We dared to slow Dale down by breaking what was otherwise an enforced code of silence. Timidly asking him to repeat or clarify his instructions only served to further fuel his rage. Roy and I were beaten for simply asking Dale for clarification, and from that point on he called us "dumbbells". It turned out to be a one-time effort.

Roy and I were not far into our first year on the northern Minnesota farm when good days without verbal assaults and beatings became increasingly rare. On other days, we stood alongside each other paralyzed with fear and frantically asking each other, "What did he say?" or "What did he mean?" before Dale's return. A dire prospect fearfully gripped my young heart. This torturous journey to which Roy and I were helplessly bound was only just beginning. Much worse, I was unaware that even greater suffering was soon to follow. We were unknowingly being led like lambs to the slaughter.

CHAPTER 3

Young Victims

Working like slaves on the farm with Dale, Roy and I had been beaten so many times that I obsessed over the subject of survival. By the time I was twelve, it was no longer possible to escape the realization that unless something was done, my brother and I would inevitably end up in the obituaries. Years later, my mother disclosed she had hoped that allowing Dale's brutal sexual abuse, which necessitated her being hospitalized several times, could somehow be used as a bargaining chip to help shield Roy and me from further abuse. Instead, suffering sexual assault gagged her with paralyzing fear, rendering her further incapable of protecting us. My mother was also silenced by the anticipation of her parents' disbelief concerning our ordeal. They would also likely voice their objection to another failed marriage. Even if our mother attempted our escape from Dale and failed, I feared for her life. I felt like a prisoner locked away in a silent dungeon. The only companions which dwelled with me were fearful thoughts of doom gnawing on my mind like rats nearly every waking moment.

The desire to escape from my imprisonment grew. One summer day, an incident occurred that triggered a scheme to kill my "jail master." Standing in a tight corner behind a loaded hay trailer, I was directing Dale with hand signals as he backed it into the hayshed. Suddenly, I was about to get sandwiched in a corner between the loaded trailer backing in and the fifteen-foot-high stack of bales behind me. With space quickly disappearing, I assumed Dale would stop before it was too late. Instead, he kept backing up, ignoring my frantic hand signals and yelling for him to stop. About to be crushed to death, I panicked. Thankfully, my survival instinct kicked in; and I was somehow able to force my body down between the stacks. Shimmying down under increasing pressure, I found safety under the loaded trailer just before it came to an airtight stop. Crawling out from beneath the trailer, I was shaking with fear that quickly turned into seething anger. Even so, I did not utter a word about my near-death experience; I would assuredly have been severely beaten. This is when the biggest rat entered the dungeon of my mind. It was the first time I had to face the disturbing reality that Dale had attempted to kill me. For if he had been successful, he could have easily dismissed it as an accident. This incident revealed that Dale had crossed a dangerous point in his degeneration. I sensed that his evil, murderous attempt trumped his consideration of even losing a much-needed slave. If there ever was a time to put a survival plan into action, this was it.

Standing eight feet above Dale on the top of a haystack, I stacked bales as he threw them up to me from the loaded hay trailer below. Next to me was a fifty-pound bag of rock salt and a pitchfork. The salt was used to sprinkle between each tier of bales to help prevent the growth and spread of mold and mildew caused by excessive heat and moisture in humid conditions. Was I going to hurl down the fifty-pound bag targeting Dale's head to break his neck, or would I use the pitchfork to stab him to death? Either plan required perfect timing, a burst of strength, and exacting precision. The stakes could not be higher. Failure would mean facing his instant retaliation and my possible death. The window of opportunity came when Dale was in the perfect position, with his back facing me as he bent over to pick up another bale. I had decided to go with the pitchfork. Poised to stab him, I heard a still small voice that spoke through my anger and hatred toward Dale say, *"Don't do it!"* This gentle voice I rarely heard suggested that my relationship with God had been choked out in the hardened soil of my heart.

The following winter presented yet another opportunity to end my living nightmare. There was a bolt-action .22 rifle that I used on rare occasions for small game hunting and recreational shooting. One cold, cloudy day, Roy was lying next to me behind a snowbank off to one side of the driveway that led to the front door of the old barn. This tall berm provided strategic cover and a good vantage point to carry out a sniper mission. Being a good shooter, I was confident that I could take Dale out. As he was walking toward the barn, he was unaware that from approximately one hundred feet away his temple was centered in my gunsights. As I slowly began squeezing the trigger, I was overcome with fear. What would it be like to spend the rest of my life in prison? I quickly lowered my rifle.

As I continued to grow in size and strength, Dale's beatings became even more fierce. His blows were dealt by a man possessed with rage, morphing into a monster. My anger and hatred intensified as slaps to the face and head increasingly turned into closed fist punches. However, there was a silver lining. Roy and I had received the God-given gifts of athleticism and strength, which were further enhanced by our ongoing years of rigorous forced labor. Even though Roy was only ninety-eight pounds as a twelve-year-old, he possessed exceptional Samson-like strength. Without this divine gift, he would likely not have survived the strain of the physical abuse. In school during PE class, Roy had developed a school-wide reputation for being an unbeatable wrestler. There was a preseason all-school invitational wrestling tournament which included several area schools. Because the tournament was an all-school invitational, anyone in Roy's sixth-grade class was allowed to participate. Roy breezed through all three of his opponents, quickly pinning them to advance to the finals in the ninety-eight-pound class. The opponent left standing in the way of his tournament win was a seventeen-year-old senior. After the match began, it looked as though Roy might be capable of pulling off an incredible upset. As hope and excitement began building and ignited the crowd, many came rushing down from the bleachers, gathering around the mat while everyone cheered Roy on, roaring, "STICK HIM, ROY!" Once in the top position, Roy was able to get a headlock on his opponent with his incredible strength; and both knew it was all but over. The packed gymnasium exploded when Roy, as a twelve-year-old sixth-grader, pinned his seventeen-year-old senior opponent, who had placed high in statewide competitions for several years. As Roy looked over at the referee slapping the mat, giving him the victory, he saw the referee shaking his head, shocked with disbelief and grinning from ear to ear. As Roy received his first-place trophy, no one knew how he came to possess such exceptional strength.

Throwing around 10,000 bales of hay each year had its benefits. During my sixth-grade softball throwing contest, I tossed the softball nearly twice as far as anyone in the class. Every year from the ages of eight to fourteen, I also won a first-place trophy in the local Punt, Pass, and Kick competition. At age eleven, I was allowed to compete at a higher regional level but lost for the first time against an unusually large kid, Robert Best. He advanced through the competition until his name was announced by the late football commentator, Pat Summerall, in the Punt, Pass, and Kick Halftime Show during the 1974 Super Bowl between the Minnesota Vikings and the Miami Dolphins. If Dale had allowed me to participate at higher levels of this competition between the ages of twelve and fourteen, I believed that I would also have had a good shot at getting my name announced. Instead, Roy's and my athletic achievements upset Dale, so he put the kibosh on our aspirations to participate in other sporting activities. Moreover, it was not worth further risking my life to challenge Dale.

It was a midsummer day as I turned thirteen when I pioneered uncharted territory. While working with Dale in the garage next to the house, I dared to subtly protest a command for the first time. We were repairing the 706 tractor that was parked outside when he told me to go tend to my two-year-old half-brother, who was sitting outside the opened garage in the dirt crying. As I begrudgingly walked over to him, Dale heard my mumbling and suddenly charged me from behind. He reached around and blindsided me with a series of punches alongside my head. The initial blows spun me around, allowing

Dale to punch me in the face. Each blow caused me to stagger and stumble further backward. As I fell to the ground with serious momentum, my head ended up slamming against the rear wheel cast iron hub of the tractor. Lying there with my head pinned against the wheel, I saw sparks inside my head as Dale straddled me. With the entire weight of his two-hundred-and-fifty-pound body upon me, he continued punching with full force. Each blow doubled the impact as my head recoiled off the cast iron wheel. Thankfully, and by the timely grace of God, I heard the fading screams of my mother as she came rushing from inside the house. Seeing Dale striking me beyond consciousness emboldened her to push him off my motionless body.

Regrettably, I was not the only one who received life-threatening beatings. The following winter, Roy had been bottle-feeding a calf in the new larger dairy barn that he and I helped build next to the old barn the previous summer. The bulk tank room, walled off from the rest of the barn where the cows were stanchioned and milked, contained a one-thousand-gallon stainless steel milk tank. Roy was crouched over, bottle-feeding a newborn calf near the entrance. To achieve maximum psychological effect, Dale snuck up behind him. Roy sensed the "whoosh of the wind" as he was about to take the impact of Dale's first blow. He then bombarded Roy with punches to both sides of his head. The blows spun him around, causing him to stumble backward into the bulk tank room. Dale's final closed fist punch to Roy's face sent him tumbling into the partially filled milk tank. Thankfully, Roy somehow fell out of the tank as he passed out. When Roy regained consciousness, he had been lying on the cold concrete floor in a large pool of blood for what had seemed like several hours. He discovered that his head, face, and nose were covered with dried blood and milk. The flies were using Roy's nose like an airport runway.

Following that brutal attack, Roy suffered severe headaches, nausea, equilibrium imbalance, and insomnia for over a month. It did not take a doctor to diagnose that Roy had suffered a severe concussion. Sadly, he never received medical treatment for his injury. Roy feared reporting this incident to my mother. For if Dale were to find out, Roy surely would have been mercilessly beaten again before even recovering from the first attack. So Roy told her that an accidental fall was responsible for his injury. As bad as these life-threatening incidents were, more unspeakable acts of horrific behavior would be committed on an even grander scale by Dale in a worse and final year yet to come.

CHAPTER 4

A Monster's Madness

The summer I turned fourteen and Roy was twelve, events unfolded which resulted in us finally escaping from Dale and his barn. By that time, his insatiable appetite to commit violent acts had taken on a whole new level of grotesque brutality. Such acts could only be executed by someone steeped in deep madness and inconceivable perversion. There was an urgency to escape the monster that choked us in its grip.

Not long after Roy and I helped Dale build a larger dairy barn that could stanchion forty milk cows, the dairy operation increased from twenty-five to forty cows, almost doubling our workload. Up to forty wheelbarrow loads of manure had to be hauled out of the barn during each daily gutter cleaning. To help make life easier, Dale purchased an industrial barn gutter cleaner costing several thousand dollars. It was an assembly of paddles connected by a chain that was pulled through the manure gutter by an electric motor mounted to the top of a ramp outside the barn. As the loaded paddles of manure exited the barn and traveled up to the end of the ramp, the chain and paddles rotated around a sprocket like a chain on a bicycle. The manure was then dumped into a manure spreader parked underneath the ramp before the chain and paddles returned on a circuitous route back into the barn. Once the spreader was filled, it was pulled by a tractor into the fields to be evenly dispersed as fertilizer. The gutter cleaner, although expensive and time-consuming to install, provided much-needed relief from barn cleaning using a wheelbarrow. However, it was not long before Dale despised Roy and me for enjoying our break from barn cleaning the hard way. To Dale, we were undeserving and needed to be punished. Within a few weeks, he deviously left the barn cleaner service disconnect switch in the off position, much to our dismay. I feared being severely beaten if I flipped the switch back on without Dale's approval, and so our slave labor continued.

As the cows were rounded up and brought into the barn for milking, there were times when one resisted being stanchioned and became the object of Dale's unleashed savagery. After the problem cow was finally secured in its stanchion, it was unable to escape from what Dale believed was deserved discipline. With Copenhagen juice spewing out of his mouth, yelling and vehement cussing were a warning that the stage was being set to execute his barbaric treatment. Dale yelled his often-used statement in blistering rage, "I'm going to teach you a lesson!" Then he grabbed his favorite instrument of torture, a pitchfork, and forcefully jabbed and scraped the cow numerous times. The manure-coated tines deeply penetrated its hindquarters. Deep furrows were raked over the cow's entire back, drawing blood. While being subjected to such intense pain, the cow displayed the whites of its eyes before dropping to its knees, bellowing loud guttural blood-curdling grunts. This torture caused profuse bleeding. To maximize the intensity and duration of the cow's suffering, Dale withheld antibiotics and other treatment, which further inflamed the cow's back and hindquarters for weeks, causing acute infection. Other times, Dale grabbed a hammer and forcefully struck the cow on the forehead until it collapsed. Tragically, some cows, unable to escape the trauma by immediate death, exhibited irregular behavior consistent with permanent brain damage. For this reason, the hammer was Dale's second favorite torture tool of choice after the pitchfork, only because replacing cows bludgeoned to death was costly.

Continuing to further sink into a dark abyss of insanity, Dale occasionally jabbed and raked furrows of blood over all forty cows stanchioned in the barn. His fits of madness typically lasted over an hour and left pools of blood. Finally, Dale took a break in the barn, saturated in sweat and utterly exhausted. Individual cows suffering was sickening enough, but watching dozens of cows undergo such savage brutality was traumatizing. To help preserve my sanity, I walked away from the barn and the sight of such wickedly spawned acts of grotesque brutality. I distanced myself beyond earshot of the horrendous sound of so many animals undergoing unspeakable torture and pain.

If Dale's torturous savagery was not cruel enough, the most dramatic and demonically inspired act he committed was yet to come. He was aware that my brother, Roy, demonstrated a profound love for horses and, as a gifted artist, could sketch beautiful renderings of them in outdoor settings. Two years later, Roy's eighth-grade art teacher referred him to a group of professional artists from California. Expressing their astonishment for such talent at his young age, they encouraged Roy to share his artistic gift with the rest of the world. The artists had such high hopes for him that they offered their assistance to help him develop his art career. They offered Roy a full-ride scholarship once he graduated from high school.

Dale despised acts of love tenderly expressed toward objects of affection. Therefore, the demented reasoning in his warped mind permitted Roy to buy a horse. He was twelve when Dale took him to buy his first horse at a local stockyard. This fresh target would provide the greatest opportunity to rip apart Roy's heart.

I was excited to share in Roy's joy as he returned with his new horse that he affectionately named Ginger. It was a fitting name for this beautiful buckskin horse. As Roy arrived back home, it was clear that Ginger was very young and not yet halter broken. Setting up a devious trap, Dale deliberately left the scene, leaving Roy without a ramp to safely unload his filly from the slippery pickup bed. Dale was fully aware that there was a hazardous three-foot drop to the ground. Ginger lost her footing multiple times and resisted Roy's efforts to help her leap out of the truck. A long struggle ensued between Roy and his horse. I was troubled as I realized that Dale had successfully set the stage for a struggle between Roy and Ginger. It was clear that this trap was perpetrated so that Dale could justify teaching another one of his sinister lessons.

Just as expected, Dale returned to intervene. The lesson he was about to teach Roy would never be forgotten. Clearly, Dale's motive was to show Roy and Ginger who was boss. Dale was also overdue for a sick fix that would pump his body full of uncontrollable rage. Without a ramp, he knew that Roy's horse would be uncooperative without a safe way to get down.

One unsuccessful attempt to get Ginger out of the truck was enough to trigger Dale's diabolical metamorphosis. Venomous anger began flowing through his body, causing blood vessels to bulge out of his neck and forehead. Dale began to spiral further out of control. Ginger, also sensing his transformation, revealed the whites of her eyes; and her body increasingly quivered with mounting fear.

As this scenario unfolded, the vicious cycle of Dale's anger and subsequent reactions that were about to take place was predictable. Ginger's natural reaction of fear and resistance would increase proportionately to Dale's escalating rage. A second and final unsuccessful attempt to force Roy's horse out of the truck created the intense drama necessary to make Dale's predictable transformation complete. The monster living within him raised its voice and yelled, "I'll fix you!"

Dale abruptly left and then quickly returned with his 706 tractor and a log chain. Then he backed up to the truck. Dale jumped off the tractor to hook one end of the log chain around Ginger's neck and the other end of the chain to the tractor hitch. Walking toward the house to escape the madness, I turned and saw Dale yank Ginger by the neck out of the truck with the tractor. Roy and my mother remained standing at the scene, shocked into silence as they watched Dale pull the filly down the driveway toward the gravel road.

Large fields on both sides of the road provided a half-mile-long open view of Ginger trying to keep up as she galloped behind the tractor. In fourth gear at full throttle, the 706 reached a maximum speed of 30 miles per hour. Past the half-mile vantage point, I heard the sound of the tractor's roar fade as it sped down a hill and out of sight. From inside the house on what had been an otherwise rare, calm summer day, I heard the tractor returning to the farm. As Dale approached the intersection of the road and driveway, he slowed down, turning the tractor around to repeat his torturous route with Ginger struggling to keep up.

For over an hour, Dale made several trips up and down the road at high speed with Ginger in tow at full gallop. Searching for some elusive peace inside the house, I was troubled by the ominous feeling that a torturous and terrifying end for Ginger was drawing near. Suddenly, the shocking sounds of my mother's bloodcurdling screams and Roy's loud wailing rattled me. Rushing outside, I witnessed an inconceivably evil spectacle unfold. As I dared to look down the road, I saw the tractor roar toward my mother, Roy, and me. Yet I was unable to see Ginger until I noticed that she had collapsed and was being pulled on her side over the gravel at full speed. I was shocked as Dale came to the intersection of the driveway, turned around, and continued while Ginger was being skinned alive. With the will to fight for her life, she repeatedly struggled to regain her footing. Tragically, one last fall flipped Ginger over; the gravel freshly ripped apart her other side, hastening her brutal death. I felt desperately helpless watching this precious filly frantically kick for her life.

As Dale made several more trips up and down the road, Ginger kicked less and less, a sign that she was succumbing to horrific wounds and approaching a horrendous end. When he saw that Ginger was nearing death, he pulled the dying horse into the driveway. He dumped her in front of the house where we stood in utter shock and disbelief. This is when the monster inside Dale could feed on watching Roy witness Ginger gasp her final breath.

Roy's spirit was broken, likely scarring his soul for life. He collapsed next to his beloved horse, which he had always dreamed of owning, his hopes dashed. As Roy gave Ginger his final farewell, he embraced Ginger's neck, trying to ignore her exposed rib cage and gravel-filled flesh. Mustering her last bit of strength, she lifted her head just long enough to look up at Roy. The whites of Ginger's eyes told one brief final story of unimaginable fear and pain. Finally, death came to claim her as she slowly released her last futile breath. Roy began wailing over Ginger, his face contorted with indescribable agony. My mother kneeled alongside them to share in the depth of Roy's pain.

Suddenly, a violent rage yanked me into uncharted emotional territory. I ran over to Dale as he climbed off the tractor and yelled, "What the heck is wrong with you?" As his feet touched the ground, I got in Dale's face with my fists raised to beat him to death. My rage stunned Dale, and he froze. Staring him in the face was the yearling ox who had grown and now posed a threat. After Dale quickly sized me up, he turned and walked away in defeat. At that moment, a dramatic shift in my perception of him took place. As Dale walked out of sight, it was as if I saw the man behind the curtain and recognized him as an absolute coward. All the cemented fear of Dale that had imprisoned me instantly crumbled, and I was set free by this moment of truth. Although still psychotic and evil, he was no longer a larger-than-life all-powerful monster. Finishing out that final summer living under Dale's roof, I never spoke to or worked for him again. My mother warned him that I was planning to kill him. Taking my threat seriously, Dale left me alone.

Released from the constant fear of being beaten, I was consumed with plotting how to exact my revenge and take Dale's life. Day and night, I considered countless scenarios of how, when, and where I could attack him. Would I surprise him from behind like he had done with Roy and me and beat Dale to death with my hands? Would I bludgeon him with a hammer just like he had done with the cows? What about shooting Dale in the head… but not before I took pleasure in watching him beg for his life on his knees? My new obsession proved I was free… or was I?

Thankfully, my mother felt compelled to help keep me separated from Dale. Even so, another problem emerged. Drinking the same potent elixir of hatred and rage that Dale drank, I was developing an unquenchable thirst for its intoxicating effects. I was morphing into the likeness of someone I hated more than anyone in the world. The enemy's evil plan to poison my soul with hatred and bitterness was working remarkably well. "The thief [the devil] comes only to steal and kill and destroy" (John 10:10a).

Even though Roy continued to do chores, a revolutionary resistance against Dale also began brewing inside of him. As Roy fed the cattle in the lot behind the barn, it was also the place where Dale chose to leave Ginger's carcass to rot. The decaying horse was strategically left leaning up against the gate inside the fenced cattle lot. Roy was forced to walk over it and through a pile of crawling maggots while battling hordes of flies on his way to the feed trough twice daily. Dale even tolerated the foul stench that permeated the stagnant summer air hovering over the farm like a thick fog. This way the monster within Dale could relish in Roy's ongoing psychological torment. Several months passed before Dale responded to our mother's incessant pleading to tow the horse carcass to wooded pastureland far away from the buildings.

My mother felt sorry for Roy. She understandably wanted him to have another horse. However, receiving Dale's approval required audacity and cunning. My mother's pitch would focus on relieving him of his displeasure of having to round up milk cows twice a day on foot, especially when the cows grazed in distant pastures. So she proposed that Roy could round up the cows on horseback. Dale accepted my mother's proposal, and Roy was allowed to own another horse. He named her Beauty.

When the new horse arrived, Dale chose a formerly used corn crib and the most rat-infested building on the farm to provide boarding. Cavernous cracks under and through the cement foundation allowed for a high volume of rodent traffic to gain access into the structure. Beneath the building existed a vast array of interconnected underground tunnels used by a highly active unfathomable rat population. Relentless nightly attacks from this army of rats began eating Beauty alive bite by bite, exposing fresh gnaw marks on Roy's horse nearly every morning. With other safer places to board Beauty, Dale's reasoning for choosing this specific building was driven by a deliberate and nefarious motive. Unlike the horrifically quickened death of Ginger, having more time to execute a slower and subtler approach to Beauty's torture provided yet another way for the monster living inside of Dale to savor a sadistic experience. Thankfully, however, Beauty's life would be rescued.

Roy took the matter of protecting Beauty literally into his own hands. One day, my brother was lying on the ground; I was shocked to find him reaching with his arms fully extended into the enormous holes. I was even more aghast as I witnessed Roy spend hours fearlessly yanking out rats the size of small dogs by their tails. He swung the rats around by their tails and dashed their heads up against the side of the structure. Roy tossed the rats behind the building which created a large mound of rats. It was miraculous that he did not get bitten after his weeklong mission of killing dozens of rats. One by one, each rat killed represented what Roy wanted to do to Dale. It was an exercise that helped Roy relieve pent-up emotions.

Our day of deliverance we had long hoped for finally came. Dale instructed Roy to burn the garbage in the ravine, keeping the fire far away from heaping piles of tires. Dozens of tires catching ablaze would send up a huge billowing cloud of smoke that could be seen for miles and attract unwanted attention. By this time, Dale had crossed a line with Roy concerning both of his horses, and now it was payback time. Defiantly, Roy deliberately set the tires on fire. When Dale saw the towering inferno spewing pitch-black smoke high into the sky and shading the sun, he came rushing out of the barn. With Roy nowhere to be found, Dale stormed toward the house. Roy was watching out the kitchen window. He knew Dale would be coming for him. This was it. Roy quickly alerted my unsuspecting mother, who was standing with her back turned, washing dishes at the kitchen sink. Just before Dale charged into the house, she yelled, "Run for your life!" Roy escaped out the back door and ran down the driveway into a freshly cut forty-acre hayfield on the other side of the road. Grabbing a thick cast iron frying pan, my mother firmly held it with both hands, planting her feet in the middle of the kitchen, poised like a batter in a batter's box. As Dale stormed into the kitchen, he saw my mother and attempted to punch her in the face without heeding the object that she was holding. He was met with a preemptive cast iron lights-out blow to the head that dropped him to the floor. Regrettably, Dale quickly recovered and then struck my mother's face with his fist. She fell, unconscious. Stepping over my mother's motionless body, Dale ran out the door, continuing his pursuit. However, Roy could run much faster than him; so the chase quickly ended. Looking back at Dale from the middle of the field, Roy hoped that he would survive to see yet another day.

Returning to the house, I was shocked to see my mother frantically loading everyone up in the station wagon. I could sense that something had gone terribly wrong, yet she refused to talk to me. If my mother had told me about Dale's attack on her, he would have been a dead man. It was ironic as we drove away fleeing for our lives that we experienced such unfamiliar peace. Watching the black smoke fade from view and leaving what looked like a war zone, I anticipated a new life in which the atrocities in the barn would quickly be forgotten. How mistaken I was with the twists and turns awaiting me on the troubling road ahead.

CHAPTER 5

Wayward Bound

After my mother finally found the courage to leave northern Minnesota with my four brothers and me, Roy and I went to live with our biological father; life took a nonthreatening turn. I began my freshman year in high school and Roy, his first year in junior high. Our father was remarried with three more children. He lived on a small, inactive five-acre farm fifteen miles away from Winnebago, Minnesota, near the unincorporated town of Northrup. My father was a long-haul truck driver gone throughout the workweek transporting mobile homes.

My mother and three younger half-brothers stayed with my grandparents, Hap and Pearl. Unbelievably, a few months later, she risked her life by returning to Dale with the three younger boys. Within a short time, my mother witnessed Dale toss their three-year-old son across the bulk tank room in the new barn. My little brother bounced off the wall, landing on the concrete floor unconscious. This incident prompted my mother to finally leave Dale and never return. She filed for divorce. To protect his million-dollar-plus net worth, Dale lawyered up. My mother ended up forfeiting a substantial financial settlement in order to gain full custody of my half-brothers and avoid a protracted legal battle. She then bought a small house in Winnebago. She worked at the local cannery and later as a home health aide providing home care for the elderly and disabled. In addition, my mother was also an evening cook at a nursing home in town. My mother's hard work ethic was a powerful testament to her strength and resolve to rebuild a better life from the ash heap for her children.

Once again, my mother and father both lived in the same area where I was born. When I was between the ages of fourteen and eighteen, Roy and I were shuffled back and forth between our parents. Thankfully, and in stark contrast to living with Dale, my father genuinely cared for Roy and me. The setting he provided offered relative peace and a desperately needed reprieve from my previous hostile environment. Living with our father, Roy and I were able to enjoy ample recreational activities such as camping and motorcycling in the summers. During the winters, we participated in radar runs, which were quarter-mile snowmobile drag races on the frozen lakes in the region. My father, along with extended family and friends, purchased the fastest sleds available. After we modified the gearing, Roy, with his lighter frame, was the designated driver; and we won many races. We had an abundance of fun, and the change could not have been more refreshing. Furthermore, Roy and I were able to enjoy our close relationship forged from the tremendous suffering we had endured together.

However, after surviving six years of ongoing trauma, hatred and bitterness had taken their toll; and my relationship with God was practically nonexistent. My disposition further deteriorated while living with a father who was immoral and exposed me to a new set of corrosive values and circumstances.

Living in this new home environment, I found dark forces changed tactics and were now more subtle and enticing. My father encouraged putting my manhood to the test through drinking and exploring carnal adventures. Leading by example, he outdrank and held his liquor better than anyone I knew. My father was also unfaithful to his second wife, just as he had been to my mother. He impressed upon me that the number of women slept with defined the identity and measure of a man. This notion, also shared by those who were like-minded in my father's tight-knit circle of extended family and friends, deeply influenced me. Hooked by these new obsessions, powerful winds blew my spiritual ship further off course toward a rocky reef.

Throughout high school, I worked for my grandfather Hap and two uncles. They owned a multigenerational farm with several thousand acres of cropland spread throughout the county. I found hard work much more enjoyable when no longer being brutally beaten like a slave. In the summers, I hand-weeded soybean fields, which, according to local vernacular, was referred to as bean walking. In the fall, I worked several hours after school plus fourteen to sixteen hours a day on weekends plowing and disking numerous fields of up to two hundred acres. I genuinely liked fieldwork operating large tractors, including a dual-wheeled, four-wheel-drive unit. Inside the cab, I especially enjoyed the stereo blaring Casey Kasem's *American Top 40* and favorite hits such as Al Stewart's "Time Passages" and Ambrosia's "How Much I Feel."

As a sixteen-year-old six-foot-one sophomore, I weighed one hundred ninety-five rock-solid pounds with seventeen-inch biceps. I could bench press the entire stack of weights in the Winnebago High School weight room. I was the strongest student of all the junior and senior athletes. Since my last name is Hill, I was nicknamed "Hillbaum" after the stout strength and conditioning coach, Mr. Bierbaum. Beyond reaping the physical benefit of years of hard labor, I engaged in weightlifting and bodybuilding. My exercise regimen was a futile effort in finding something that I could like about myself and to find relief for pent-up hatred and bitterness.

One time during the summer between my sophomore and junior years, I was weightlifting at my mother's house when I vaguely heard a familiar voice through my bedroom door. It was Dale! Adrenaline and rage surged through my body. Rushing to the kitchen where Dale was seated, I picked up where we had left off from our confrontation two years earlier. I did not want to beat him to death in front of my mother, so I taunted him to join me outside and to "take it like a man." Dale boiled over with instantaneous fury, but fear kept him from standing up. Hovering over him I yelled that if I ever saw him under different circumstances, he would be a dead man. Even though this was the last time I ever saw Dale, the lingering impact of his evil torture triggered deep-seated anger.

By the time I was a senior, the high school football coach had been pleading with me for two years to join the varsity football team. He told me that with my powerful build and physicality, I could be an All-American running back. However, I was cursed with many lies placed upon me by Dale and his monster. My soul wore the label "dumbbell" that had been beaten into me, and I believed that I was unloved and deplorable. In addition to self-hatred, my distrust and unre-solved bitterness prevented me from being on any team. Therefore, it just seemed easier to deal with my disposition by being a loner, especially at school. Every time the coach approached me, I wrote him off. To make sure he got my message, I acted like an idiot foolishly displaying acts of blatant defiance. For example, when we had soccer in his PE class, I deliberately perturbed the coach, sabotaging my teammates as I scored goals against them, causing them to lose. Afterward, when anyone asked what the heck was wrong with me, I dared them to do something about it. Instead of reaching out for help, I pushed everyone away. Contrary to acting out, I actually yearned for someone to unconditionally love me through my woundedness and lead me on a path to inner healing.

Upon graduation from high school, I attained the full-fledged status of a weekend warrior and became a womanizer just like my father. If more noble goals were ever to be aspired to, I didn't care in the slightest to go after them. Like a rudderless ship, I was hopelessly adrift. My father, a Marine veteran, encouraged me to enlist in the Marine Corps. Lacking vision, I signed up, if not for any other reason than to impress him.

After flying into the Marine Corps Recruit Depot in San Diego, California, from Minneapolis, Minnesota, I began Basic Training. It wasn't long before I was noticed for achieving perfect physical fitness scores and was selected as a platoon leader. Because of my position, I was granted immunity from the wrath of my drill instructors. Most of the time, I stood alongside them as they yelled threats and insults at my fellow recruits. I chuckled inside thinking that these tactics, which caused some recruits to shake in their boots and one to have a nervous breakdown, were harmless compared to Dale's. As for knowing what "mean" really looked like, I had somehow endured six years of Hell akin to a POW camp. Surviving torture from a psychotic grandmaster in the highest rank of mean, my brutal experience with Dale had desensitized and hardened me. I even discovered that turning on "mean" like a switch was pleasurable.

During Basic Training, a recruit with a runaway loud mouth lipped off and irritated our platoon. In one particular hand-to-hand combat training class, our platoon was paired up. One of the drill instructors made sure that, as platoon leader, I was matched up with this problematic recruit. Everyone knew the reason why. When training began, I immediately took him down to the mat using a rear-naked chokehold. I deliberately applied more pressure than necessary, causing him to pass out. As the recruit lay motionless, training was suspended to allow for medical personnel to arrive on the scene to revive him. After the recruit was released from the medical bay and returned to the barracks, he was uncharacteristically quiet and compliant throughout the remainder of Boot Camp. An incident that should have sparked an investigation otherwise served to further solidify my status as the top recruit in Basic Training.

Graduating from Basic Training, I was selected as a Platoon Leader, Series, and Company Honorman, which were the top honors out of all one thousand recruits. I was awarded these honorary titles and therefore promoted to Private First Class in the presence of the Marine Corps Commandant. Having coped with Dale's extreme torture, mental and physical hardships turned into advantages by the grace of God. "You intended to harm me, but God intended it for good to accomplish what is now being done" (Genesis 50:20a).

Returning home on leave between Basic Training and my first assigned duty station, I anticipated my father, a Marine vet, would be proud of my achievement. His praise and affirmation would have been my greatest reward of all. Instead, I was emotionally deflated when my father's reaction was curiously indifferent. Several days later, I discovered the reason why. Visiting my grandparents while I was home, Hap confirmed that my father was notoriously wild and rebellious as a teenager. He told me that after my father turned fifteen and had begun dating my mother, he faced serious trouble stemming from illegal drag racing. To avoid being arrested, he had evaded the law in several hot pursuits; and his license was revoked. Even so, my father defiantly continued to race, landing in jail with his car permanently impounded. After he was released, his blatant disrespect for the law continued. During one incident, he initiated a physical confrontation with the Winnebago police chief. My father started a scuffle during which he ripped off the chief's badge and threw it on the ground. My father continued taunting the police chief with the family's horse named Billy. Several times he rode the horse into Winnebago despite implicit orders not to, showboating his defiance on horseback while being chased several times by law enforcement. My father's favorite part of his escapades was being cheered on by the townsfolk who came out of storefronts to watch him gallop by as he rode out of town. Although he never got caught, he was issued a unique ultimatum by the local authorities. My father was given the choice of serving behind bars or serving in the Marine Corps. As he chose the latter option, he was bussed off to enlist. My father's parents and also law enforcement were hoping that he would finally get straightened out.

I was surprised, however, when my grandfather, Hap, shared a final detail that very few knew. He informed me that my father had been issued an early military discharge for non-compliant conduct. This previously missing piece of information connected the dots, and then it all made sense. Because of my father's nature, my accomplishment aroused his jealousy. I had been naïve in believing that putting a lot of sweat equity into Boot Camp would make him proud of me. Instead, my father's indifference was devastating. Taking a direct hit from the bullet of rejection penetrated deeply into my soul, and I felt more disillusioned and worthless than ever.

My first duty station was Marine Corps Air Station New River in Jacksonville, North Carolina. While stationed there, I was required to serve one six-month Mediterranean deployment. Naturally adventurous, I volunteered to go on a second overseas tour. After both deployments, I was able to fly throughout Europe as a CH-53 Sea Stallion helicopter crew member. The list of countries I visited included Portugal, Spain, Great Britain, Norway, France, Italy, Greece, Turkey, Belgium, and Lebanon. From the helicopter, I was able to capture extraordinary aerial views while flying over such places as the mountainous fjords of Norway and the Roman Colosseum.

In Tunisia, North Africa, I enjoyed a memorable two-week encampment with my helicopter squadron along the northern coastline. During that time, I met an inquisitive ten-year-old French-Tunisian girl. She was barefoot and wore a bright multi-striped orange, blue, and white cultural dress. The girl had long dark brown, wavy hair with olive-colored skin. Curiosity drew her to our encampment each day. I took the time and effort to befriend this Tunisian girl despite the language barrier. I placed my portable cassette tape player headphones on her head. She listened to what I was playing at the time, which was Lionel Ritchie's "Stuck on You." Fascinated, the girl grinned from ear to ear, indicating that she had never known such a device existed. As I shared portions of my military MREs (Meals Ready-to-Eat), she must have thought them tasty because every day she kept coming back for more. As the young girl left our encampment for the final time, she ran off to join a group of women dressed in similar bright clothing carrying large jugs of water on their heads. They were being led down a footpath by an old man dressed in a dirty, ragged suit coat and trousers carrying a walking stick. Encamped on this foreign shore isolated from the influences of modern times was like watching a live scene out of a *National Geographic* magazine, which I found enchanting.

Throughout my military service, I was discontent and troubled while living a double life. I brought a Bible aboard ship, where it remained stowed away beneath my bottom bunk like a good luck charm. Left unread, it still remained a powerful reminder that my life was out of alignment with God. Hoping to ease my pricked conscience aboard ship, I professed to my Marine pals the respect that I had for God. Yet on shore at various ports, I caroused the European nightlife attempting to outperform my buddies at scoring with foreign women. Aboard ship, all of my friends knew that my words promoting God were nothing more than a façade. Because on shore, my testimony was betrayed by my promiscuous deeds. In short, I fit the perfect profile of a hypocrite.

Meanwhile, at home in southern Minnesota, my brother, Roy, was also dealing with an anger-scorched soul. This led him down a path of self-destruction and violence. Roy's struggle was especially understandable when, years later, he revealed that in addition to all the beatings that I knew about, there were even more. Multiple times Dale ambushed Roy as he entered the chicken coop and mercilessly beat him for no reason. Although Roy survived the additional assaults, he was unable to escape the fear of frightening consequences should Dale ever discover that Roy had told anyone about the beatings.

While I was overseas, Roy turned sixteen and was issued his driver's license. His 1967 Ford Fairlane gave him the freedom to take a road trip on a two-year drinking binge. Roy got drunk every day that summer between his sophomore and junior years. On weekends after getting kicked out of bars for being too young, he started fights in the parking lot, sometimes with several individuals at a time. During one incident, Roy was in the parking lot of a popular bar in the neighboring town of Fairmont. Three men drove in, and one of them flipped him off. Roy left all three lying on the asphalt unconscious.

Roy was notorious for stealing cars and taking them on joyrides, yet never getting caught. He stole one car three times. Roy also broke into buildings and vandalized them. The only time he ever faced consequences for wrongdoing was when he was caught breaking into an industrial facility. Instead of going to jail, Roy worked out a deal with the building's owner to unload train cars for a month. During his junior year, he drank during school hours and beat up several students and even a male history teacher. Before Roy was permanently expelled, a healthcare professional was brought in to assess his condition. It was determined that he should be sent away for eight weeks of detox. Before walking through the second set of glass doors to check in, Roy saw many patients dressed in pajamas. This sight rattled Roy, and he immediately turned around and walked out.

Roy's deep dive into the bottle nearly landed him in a detox facility. This sobering experience compelled him to fight for a fresh start to clean up his act. So with fifty dollars in his pocket, Roy set out in his Ford Fairlane for St. Regis, Montana to join my father with his second wife and their three other children to scout out a job. Arriving to enroll at St. Regis High School to finish his junior year, he discovered the principal waiting for him with his records in hand, intending to give him the boot. Roy looked him in the eyes and convinced him that he would steer clear of drinking and stay out of trouble. Roy kept his promise. He was later chosen as prom king and, after his high school graduation, married his high school sweetheart and prom queen, WaNell. However, Roy's battle with the bottle would continue.

After serving 4 years, I was honorably discharged from the Marine Corps in 1985. I was ecstatic as I boarded a flight destined for St. Regis, Montana, where Roy, my father, and his second family had moved. Having enjoyed camping and elk hunting trips in the Rockies of western Montana with them in years past, all of us desired to relocate there one day; and I was the last one to join them. After arriving in St. Regis, I was hired by the local sawmill where Roy worked.

Meanwhile, I continued traveling down a wayward road of excessive drinking. I was desperately searching to find something or someone to fill the chasm that separated my soul from

God. This yearning led me into a relationship with a beautiful young woman named Lisa, who was the lead singer in her family's country music band. Our infatuation was immediate, and she quickly became my sole obsession. During our relationship, Lisa and I traveled throughout western Montana. She performed in all types of venues, from holes-in-the-wall to high-class resorts. For her performances, our fringe benefits included favorable treatment, hotel accommodations, and an unlimited supply of alcohol. The relationship between Lisa and I, however, barely lasted a year. She was strongly influenced by her parents, especially her father, who had performed with household names. They convinced Lisa that I was a distraction and, therefore, disadvantageous in advancing her potentially famous music career. It was ironic that I could not have agreed with them more.

This painful breakup nudged me to the edge of an emotional cliff. Numbed by the experience, I began to make some of the worst decisions of my life. Choosing to double down on a self-destructive road, I stomped my foot on the accelerator, continuing to head in the opposite direction from God. The road was about to get darker and more dangerous, with my bad choices leading me further into the unknown and deeper nether regions of the enemy's kingdom.

CHAPTER 6
Entering a Dark Kingdom

As the winter of 1986 approached, I was twenty-two when I befriended an individual whom I will refer to as Mike. He was a long-distance national track star looking to get a fresh start in St. Regis, Montana, after having attended Arizona State University. During Mike's time at ASU, he was swept up in the current of the cocaine underworld. After arriving in St. Regis, he accepted a guest speaker role for a national anti-drug awareness program for area school assemblies. Mike believed that his participation in this noble cause would be an avenue of escape to help him clean up his act. However, he drank excessively like me to help provide relief from his personal demons. As we partied together on the weekends, Mike soon slipped back into the white rapids of cocaine.

Mike introduced me to a group of four young men who worked for an electric company. They erected the largest high-voltage power transmission towers in the Pacific Northwest. The crew was tight-knit, trusting each other with their lives. They worked together in a high-risk job at heights of several hundred feet around lethal amounts of electricity. These men were prolific cocaine users and most likely heavy hitters in cocaine trafficking. My interaction with this group was limited to drinking parties. I had no interest in using cocaine. My disdain for drugs began after I was offered marijuana in high school. It made me feel anxious and paranoid, so my experimentation with it was short-lived.

Nonetheless, I befriended one guy from the group nicknamed Thumper. As our friendship quickly developed, we competed against each other in one-on-one basketball in the local high school gym. Even though Thumper was a couple of inches shorter than me, he could dunk the ball. I was impressed with his power and athleticism. I was also intrigued by the license plates on Thumper's new truck that proudly bore his nickname, Thumper. This name stemmed from his notorious fighting reputation and as someone who enjoyed beating up one or several guys at once when he got high on cocaine.

It was also during this time that my other friend, Mike, introduced me to a woman named Bo. She was twenty-six, beautiful, and her form was pleasing. Her long flowing jet-black hair accentuated her dark piercing eyes. Bo looked like an Egyptian princess. Her alluring appearance was strangely mysterious in a spiritually dark sort of way. Like my other newfound acquaintances, Bo was also involved with the underworld. Yet, she possessed more direct and potent spiritual connections as a witch, well-versed in the performance of the dark arts.

Bo and I took an immediate interest in each other, and our chemistry quickly developed and led us into a close relationship. She was a palm reader. Incredibly, Bo was able to produce tangible demonstrations of raw satanic power. There were occasions when I bore witness to her supernatural manifestations. One time when we were at a local bar, Bo asked me, "Do you want to see something?" While looking at her, I noticed her eyes roll back; and she entered into a trance. Bo walked over to the nearest jackpot machine. As if it were under a mechanical spell, the machine landed on "*Jackpot*" multiple times, spitting out coinage into a white bucket until it was filled. After I observed several more similar occurrences, it was unquestionable that something beyond mere coincidence was responsible for Bo's success.

Later at the same bar, Bo cued me to observe something even more powerful. Once again she entered into a trance. The next event I witnessed was eerily strange and intense. Everyone in the bar became caught up in a fight. As if some devilish directive was issued from hell, bar patrons suddenly drew their knives and began swinging away. Others threw their glasses at each other. After the violence subsided, almost everyone was injured and or bleeding. Yet Bo and I had been left alone and without any threat of being harmed. Everyone was thrown out, and the bar was shut down.

As a palm reader, Bo gave me an interesting reading contrary to any she had given before. Most, if not all, of her readings comprised of future events containing various degrees of misfortune. With my reading, however, Bo predicted I would be given a successful and blessed life. After she gave this reading, Bo was visibly shaken and seemed confused. This foreshadowed other more profound events between her and me.

A month or so into our relationship, Bo's captivating beauty and mysterious nature ignited my desire to have a sexual relationship with her. In response to my advances, indecisiveness overcame her; and she ultimately rejected them all. At the time, I found Bo's position perplexing. I sensed that we shared the same desire; however, she steadfastly refused to yield. Looking back, I now realize that with Bo's powerful tether to the realm of darkness, a sexual bond between us would have created for me a spiritually devastating demonic soul tie. Because of her palm reading that my life would be blessed, Bo was leery of breaching a divine boundary that protected me. Ultimately, it was by the grace of God that I was prohibited from unknowingly opening a dark door that could have led to my spiritual demise.

Even though divine intervention spared me from a negative spiritual fate, the road I was on took yet an even darker turn. Bo invited two of her friends over; and upon our introduction, I stood before two men who were demon-possessed and manifested an otherworldly appearance. With extreme unease, I looked at these men's faces and felt a deathly dark force emanating from them. Looking back at me, their squinted serpentlike eyes and evil piercing stares sent shivers down my spine. It was no surprise that they introduced themselves as warlocks. Like Bo, they were practitioners of the dark arts. Thankfully, they stayed only briefly in order to make plans to meet up with her and me that night for a weekend Christmas party at the local bar. I had major reservations about going knowing these warlocks would be present. The notion of seeing them again was deeply unnerving. They had sold their souls to the devil. In exchange, the warlocks' brains were fried; no one appeared to be home.

Reluctantly, I arrived at the Christmas party with my friend, Mike. However, I was disappointed and surprised upon discovering that Bo had not arrived. Regrettably, both warlocks saw me and, with an evil laserlike focus, approached. They invited me to join them outside, yet something unfamiliar within was tugging at me to turn around and make haste to escape. However, as if cast under a spell, I followed the warlocks, which was one of the worst decisions of my life.

After climbing into the back seat of an old rundown car, one of the warlocks asked me if I wanted to take a hit from a bowl of pot. Apprehensively, I accepted. They took the first toke. As they passed the pipe back to me, they snickered, which prompted me to question what was in the bowl. Unassured by their reply, I quickly came up with what I thought was a foolproof backup plan. I would simply fake inhaling whatever it was and return to the bar as soon as possible. However, my self-preservation plan failed miserably. The substance was potent. A small amount must have inadvertently entered my system, and I quickly found myself reeling under a harsh drug reaction. Insisting that the warlocks tell me what was in the bowl, I knew it was probably too late. They told me that the pot was mixed with PCP, otherwise known as angel dust, one of the most dangerous hallucinogenic drugs in existence.

Somehow, I had managed to pull off an act of spectacular stupidity by willfully disregarding neon signs flashing, "*Warning!*" and "*Danger!*" My last intelligible thought was, *Great...you are about to forever slip away into a living nightmare with a fried brain and join these warlocks as your eternal roommates.* I felt as though I was hopelessly handcuffed to the seat of a runaway train heading into a black tunnel. The devil, wearing a billed hat as my tour guide, stood at the front of the car with an evil smile, snarling and staring back at me. Terrified, I did not want my life to be snuffed out like this. My final hope was that God would see my fast-approaching mental trainwreck and mercifully rescue me.

Within moments, I felt as though I was going insane. I ran back inside the bar and frantically grabbed my friend, Mike. Seeing something was terribly wrong, he responded without hesitation. Mike took me to his place, and for a full week I was bedridden on my friend's living room couch. Tormented with anxiety, disorientation, and short-term memory loss, I was left stranded in mental anguish, helplessly unable to perform even the simplest tasks. Turning a showerhead on and off seemed overwhelmingly complicated and nearly impossible to remember.

My dreadful state felt terminal. In my distress, I asked Mike what he thought had happened to me. I desperately yearned for a response that would provide hope. He asked me what I had taken. I told Mike about the warlocks and how they had deceived me with a bowl of pot laced with angel dust. Even if he were to lie, I would have preferred an answer such as, "It's temporary, and you'll get better." Instead, Mike told me that I might have permanently damaged my brain and could end up in a psychiatric ward. The serious look on Mike's face reflected his grave concern.

For an entire week, which seemed like a lifetime, I continued to suffer profound mental impairment. Each day Mike checked in to see how I was doing as I lay motionless on the couch in a pseudo-vegetative state. Gradually, my sense of well-being began to return, igniting hope. After recovering enough to rejoin the land of the living, one would think that my horrific experience with angel dust would spin me around in the opposite direction toward sanity. But for some inexplicable reason, I was not quite ready to take the off-ramp and reverse course just yet.

CHAPTER 7

Point of No Return

After I recovered from my disastrous trip on PCP, Mike, my track star friend, invited me to join him at a cocaine party on New Year's Eve, which was a few days away. It was an invitation offered only to those who were the region's biggest cocaine dealers. Because of my connection to Mike, I would be the lone exception. The party would take place at a private residence owned by the largest cocaine dealer, who supplied Thumper and his crew.

The reason Mike invited me to this exclusive party was that one week prior to my PCP nightmare, I joined him in jumping off a cocaine cliff, not just once, but twice. The first time was a casual and harmless one-time experiment…or so I thought. The high was so surprisingly pleasurable and powerful that I thought it wouldn't hurt to go ahead and try the white stuff for a second time only. Therein lies the illusion.

Mike was so excited that I was not only a close friend but could now be considered a coke-snorting partner that he thought a special celebration was in order. Risking his newly established important cocaine connection, Mike received approval for my invitation to this private party. Upon finding out that Thumper was also invited, I accepted.

The price of joining Mike in my experimentation with cocaine came at a high personal cost. Before enlisting in the Marine Corps, I had shot a seven-by-six-point trophy bull elk just outside Yellowstone Park in Montana with Roy and my father. Before heading home to Minnesota, a Montana game warden weighed it at 750 pounds. He said it was the largest bull harvested to date in the 1981 Montana hunting season. Before returning home to Minnesota, we strapped the enormous bull elk with its majestic antlers to the roof of our horse trailer. Making our first stop at McDonald's in Bozeman, Montana, we were quickly swarmed by a Greyhound busload of passengers and restaurant patrons coming over to stare at the bull. There was such a large crowd I felt I could've charged tickets for admission. Throughout our 1,200-mile journey home, this huge elk captivated the attention of interstate travelers; and truckers' CB radios filled the airwaves with congratulations.

When my father, Roy, and I arrived home, we were welcomed by the entire Hill family clan and some of my father's friends. A huge banner stretched the width of our farm shop, which read, "Congratulations, David, on the Imperial Elk!" Bursting with pride, I envisioned my bull elk mount would be displayed over a fireplace and admired by future generations.

No one, especially myself, would have imagined selling my prize trophy elk mount; but regretfully, that is what I did. Not even being subjected to waterboarding could have forced a confession that I had sold it to get high on cocaine. Understandably, selling the mount caused a relational rift between my father, Roy, and me. Years later, Roy and I made several attempts to recover the elk mount; yet it was never found. To this day, it is still painful to reflect upon my regretful actions.

On New Year's Eve, December 31, 1986, with a few hundred dollars' worth of cocaine left over from several days before and extra cash in my pocket from the elk sale, Mike and I jumped into my F250 pickup truck. We were headed deep into the mountains twenty miles northwest of St. Regis, Montana, to attend this exclusive cocaine "convention." Those of us invited thought we were going to a party to splurge on virtually endless lines of white powder. Instead, we were unaware that we were destined for a supernatural encounter with an almighty God. Little did we know, a sequence of miraculous events was about to unfold that would forever change our lives.

It was about 10:00 p.m. when Mike and I drove into a circular driveway well-lit against a dark winter sky. The crisp air was exceptionally quiet and still as we arrived at the cocaine party. Parked among the vehicles were the latest model Corvette and a new truck with license plates bearing Thumper's name. I paused, admiring the residence owned by a large cocaine supplier who undoubtedly made bank providing the region with large quantities of expensive white powder. The beautiful, large multi-level home was neatly tucked away on a heavily forested property that kept it well-hidden. As I climbed a long staircase with several landings, I thought this wasn't the kind of group that I preferred to hang out with. I started to feel uneasy.

Entering the second story of the house with Mike leading the way, we walked into a large vaulted living room. On the left side, there was a huge wraparound sofa that could seat a dozen or more people. Centered in front of it was a large glass coffee table. Seated between a few individuals, Thumper was forming long lines of cocaine on the glass with a razor blade. Glancing up and glad to see me, he informed me that fifteen grand in coke was to be enjoyed; and I was welcome to as much of it as I desired. Barely finishing his statement, Thumper reached for a straw and began snorting up white powdery lines.

However, my unenthusiastic reaction to Thumper's cocaine offer was out of character; and I didn't know why. I stood motionless holding my beer as Mike walked over to engage a group of individuals, including one whom I guessed was the host. Everyone was conversing under the low volume of soft rock music while I stood by myself. After some time, I realized that I had not walked far from the threshold from where I had entered, and I felt out of place. My awkwardness turned into mounting tension the longer I stood alone. Thankfully, no one had seemed to notice. As this tense feeling overwhelmed me, I needed to find a quiet place to think some things through. I turned around, seeking the privacy of the kitchen. Sitting alone at the table, I realized my life had deteriorated like my stale beer.

With a different set of eyes, I looked at my cherished companion that I was holding. My fondness for alcohol that had begun at age fifteen, and the self-indulgent experiences all over the world that it provided, suddenly faded. My thoughts deepened, bringing with them more enlightenment. I was spinning out of control, hooked on a newly acquired taste for cocaine just after miraculously dodging permanent brain damage from angel dust. Grave concerns surfaced about my destination. I shuddered to think that my life was in shambles as I gazed upon the stale beer that I continued to hold in my hand. Suddenly, I realized that for most of my life, alcohol had been a destructive force and had become a bondage from which I feared I might need deliverance.

Further reflection took me back to one morning when I awoke following my Honorable Discharge from the Marine Corps in November 1985. I had no clue as to how I had totaled my brand new truck the night before. Then, within the span of two months, I was charged with a DUI, followed by driving with an open container. For the latter conviction, I earned a free night's stay in a barred room dressed in an orange jumpsuit and was given six months' probation.

As if I was not in enough trouble, I continued drinking on weekdays well into the evenings after working long strenuous hours at the sawmill. Every weekend, I drove all over western Montana with Lisa, my band singer girlfriend, in another new truck and partied until early morning. Racing seventy-five miles from her place back to the sawmill every Monday morning with only a couple of hours' sleep, I thought I was impervious to the effect of heavy drinking and sleep deprivation. However, consequences caught up with my irresponsible lifestyle, proving my perceived invincibility a delusion. Within two weeks of signing my vehicle loan, I flipped and rolled my new truck several hundred feet down a mountainside. Even the first responders were shocked to find that Lisa and I had climbed out of the flattened cab without even a scratch.

While staring at my can of beer, I was pierced to the heart by an ultimate truth. I recognized that I was a full-blown out-of-control alcoholic. Along with this scorching revelation came a terrorizing question, one I felt helplessly unable to answer, *"How could I be freed from this powerfully addictive vice that held me in its grip?"*

Suddenly, I was transported into a supernatural realm where I stood on a desolate road. I was surrounded by a lunar-like landscape smothered by a starless canopy. The humid and stagnant air lingered with a stench. Next to the road stood a small barren tree that was charred black by its poisonous surroundings. Everywhere I looked, I saw no sign of life. If this place could have spoken through its eerie darkness, it would have revealed that it had been forever mercilessly raped by death itself. Nearby, there were ominous-looking caves, crevices, and rocks from which I sensed evil was watching my every move. These foreboding surroundings sent shivers down my spine, and I felt scarcely able to walk. It was then that I saw a large stop sign, marking the dead end of my road. I stared at it with awe, aware that this sign was placed there by God Himself and conveyed a powerful and dire warning to me.

With all the courage I could muster, I dared to approach the stop sign curious to see what lay beyond. Coming to an abrupt cliff, I peered over its jagged edge. I sensed that I was looking into an infinitely deep dark abyss, eternally distant from a life-giving, loving God. A disturbing awareness came over me. I realized I was staring into the entrance of hell, a place that separated lost, forsaken souls from the presence of God for all eternity. Feeling the horror of this place taking ahold of me, I spun around for fear that I would slip and fall. Suddenly, I returned to the the privacy of the kitchen. What would happen in the ensuing moments would change my life forever.

CHAPTER 8

Cocaine Salvation

Grateful to be released from my horrifying experience and now safely standing in the kitchen, I could not contain myself. I broke down and wept from the depth of my soul. Because God had touched my life when I was eight years old, I instinctively cried out, "Jesus, help me!" Suddenly, a warm liquid sensation began to flow over my entire body. The experience was as real as if I were standing under a shower. The powerful sensation permeated my being. Not understanding what was happening, I tried to wipe the substance off my arms; but they didn't appear wet. As this liquid sensation continued to gently flow over my body, a comforting peace settled upon me. It was then that I realized that the blood of Jesus Christ was purifying me and healing me both inside and out. Standing there in the kitchen, I stretched out my arms toward Heaven. In the following moments of awe, I received the gift of a holy life-changing experience as Jesus' overwhelming love, joy, and peace flowed over me. As my sacred shower continued, I did not want it to end!

The cords of death entangled me, the anguish of the
grave came upon me; I was overcome by trouble and

*sorrow. Then I called on the name of the Lord: "O
Lord, save me!" The Lord is gracious and righteous;
our God is full of compassion. For You, O Lord, have
delivered my soul from death, my eyes from tears, my
feet from stumbling, that I may walk before the Lord
in the land of the living.*

— Psalm 116:3–5, 8–9

Wondering if anyone noticed what was happening to
me, I glanced around the kitchen wall into the living room.
To my surprise, everyone seemed oblivious to my experience.
Not wanting to attract attention and having to explain the
unexplainable, I slipped outside. Arriving at the bottom of the
stairs, I felt transformed by the presence of God. Walking out
onto the well-lit circular driveway, I looked up into the unusually calm and crisp midnight Montana sky. I was captivated by
large magnificently designed snowflakes feathering down from
above. Experiencing such tranquility, I sensed I was standing
on holy ground in God's presence, suspended in reverent awe.
Even though I could not see God's physical form, I felt His
presence in an inexpressibly intimate and powerful way. I
became so overwhelmed with God's glory that all I could do
was cry. I felt the weight of all the chains and shackles that had
ever bound me instantly snap free.

So if the Son sets you free, you will be free indeed.

— John 8:36

Although I had greatly sinned against God in my wayward life, now I felt inexplicable peace. He was not mad at me; God truly loved me, and everything was going to be okay. Forgiven, cleansed, and freed, I felt unimaginably better. Interrupting this profound experience with God, I tearfully whispered, "Thank You."

Suddenly, God called out my name in an audible voice saying, "David," which shocked me to the core. Yet as He spoke, I sensed God's loving heart by the tone of His voice. The gentlest and most tender voice I had ever heard revealed His desire to be my closest loving friend. God knew me better than I knew myself, having watched over me every moment of my life.

> *O Lord, You have searched me and You know me.*
> *You know when I sit and when I rise; You perceive*
> *my thoughts from afar. You discern my going out and*
> *my lying down; You are familiar with all my ways.*
> *Before a word is on my tongue You know it com-*
> *pletely, O Lord. For You created my inmost being; You*
> *knit me together in my mother's womb. All the days*
> *ordained for me were written in Your book before one*
> *of them came to be.*
>
> *— Psalm 139:1–4, 13, 16b*

At that moment, God's incredible love for me was tangible, instantly penetrating deep within my soul as a personal revelation. I was undone.

God spoke again, this time with a promise, reverent fear gripped my heart. His awesome voice projected unlimited power and authority; and I recognized Him as ruler and judge of the universe. I felt as though I was going to collapse and die. Even so, God shored me up so that I could withstand hearing Him speak, "David, you will no longer have problems with drugs or alcohol again." After hearing God's words, I knew that nothing or no one could prevent His promise from coming to fruition. Overflowing with relief and assurance, I knew this promise came from the same voice that spoke the universe into existence and commanded the daily rising and setting of the sun.

Then God spoke a second promise, "David, I am going to give you a successful life." After He spoke, I realized that I had squandered the precious life God had given me thus far on self-indulgent living. Feeling completely undeserving, I wept.

Furthermore, God spoke a third and final promise to me. It seemed as though He was saving the best for last. I sensed God's lighthearted and joyful nature and that He was delighted when He said, "I am going to give you a beautiful wife." God knew this promise was one that I had greatly anticipated and that I would receive it with an overflowing joy in my heart. He saw the loneliness and frustration that I had encountered on a futile and seemingly endless search to find the woman of my dreams. God also knew that I had paid the high cost of too many in-and-out relationships and one-night stands. These self-induced wounds afflicted my soul with sleepless nights filled with heartache. After God finished speaking, I remained suspended in profound shock and awe. Yet, only He knew my evening was just beginning. God's intention to crash the cocaine party was still on His docket.

Standing coatless in the frosty winter air, I found God's tangible and abiding presence a source of physical warmth and strength. Softly weeping, I watched large fluffy snowflakes continue to feather down from the calm midnight sky. I was awestruck by the revelation that each snowflake with its unique ornate design was created by the same God who was with me and whose voice I had just heard.

My serenity with God was interrupted by someone coming down the steps. It was Thumper. His otherwise rugged tough-guy face had a deer in the headlights look as he unknowingly walked into my interaction with God's presence. Thumper's astonished reaction would be the first of many before the night was over. Startled, he immediately asked, "What the...?" Thumper was so perplexed that he forgot to complete his question, leaving it dangling before it vaporized in the crisp midnight air. Gifted with a new set of spiritual eyes and with the assistance of God's presence, I was given insight into the activity taking place in his soul. Reading his spiritual mail, I could discern that an insatiable enslaving thirst controlled Thumper. His endless searching had led him to a dead end where Thumper tasted worldly wells that were bitter or turned up dry. I could also see that he was like low-hanging fruit ready to be picked for God. Nothing could stop me from zealously lunging toward him, driven by God's uncontainable love. Giving Thumper a bear hug and not letting go, I blurted out, "Jesus just saved me, and you can have Him too!" Continuing to squeeze him in a tight embrace, I was fully aware that Thumper enjoyed beating people up when he was high on coke. And I had just rattled him with the most offensive words he likely had ever heard. Yet, at that moment, it did not matter. Like butter sizzling in a frying pan, I was holding on to a so-called tough guy who was quickly melting. After realizing that I had embraced Thumper long enough, I released him; and he was weeping.

As Thumper stood in front of me, I noticed that he was no longer under the influence of cocaine or alcohol. Instead, he was staggering under the influence of God. When Thumper was finally able to speak, he could only muster up one thing to say. Tearfully, he said that he didn't understand what was going on but that he wanted Jesus, too. Without the benefit of a divine memo, I did not have a plan for what to do next; but I did feel inspired to take my new supercharged faith on a test run. I took hold of Thumper. Together, we walked arm in arm up the stairs, returning to the party with both of us weeping the whole way.

As God's presence arrived with Thumper and me, a silence swept through the living room, prompting a collective response. It appeared as though everyone at the party was awe-struck as they halted their activities and turned to stare at us. At that moment, I saw upward of fifteen cocaine dealers with fifteen deer in the headlights looks. Without a word, it was as if there was a prime directive issued from Heaven commanding everyone to be seated on the large circular sofa. The host turned off the music and sat down with all the others.

With tears still streaming down my cheeks, I walked over to the middle of the room and stood before everyone. Introducing myself to those whom I had yet to meet was not nearly as important as introducing God first. God released His all-consuming love and power through me, causing me to burst and share my fresh supernatural encounter with Him.

I told those seated at the party that Jesus had just saved me, and I was never going to be the same again. I offered the invitation that they could have Jesus, too. Once again, I was granted the opportunity to peer into the depth of each soul. Everyone's story was essentially the same as Thumper's; every heart desperately hungered and thirsted to be filled. All were left stranded, unsatisfied with their own vices. As God continued to pour out His love and penetrate the hearts of the attentive coke dealers seated before me, nearly everyone began weeping, repenting, and praising God. Most everyone came over to me, and a hugfest ignited. However, two men sat back, seemingly unresponsive to this powerful move of God. They were the host and my friend, Mike.

God's intervention brought the otherwise all-night party to a premature end. As some guests began leaving, I stepped away to a far corner of the living room to reflect on everything that had just taken place. It was then that God gently spoke to my heart, "*I have come to answer your mother's prayers.*" He gave me a vision of her fervently praying for me on her knees. This confirmed what I had known for many years. My mother had been burdened as she watched me become enslaved in my unforgiveness and bitterness toward Dale, my evil stepfather. As a result, she knew that I had drifted far off course from my relationship with God. Humbled, I overflowed with tears of gratitude toward my praying mother.

Suddenly, the atmosphere shifted; and I was aggressively approached by the furious host, who was accompanied by someone I assumed was his bodyguard. The host introduced himself, but it was not so we could exchange pleasantries. He pulled out a .357 handgun and pointed it at me. The host informed me that I had ruined his party. He delivered the warning that unless I left the premises immediately, he was going to kill me. During the confrontation, Mike rushed over to de-escalate the situation. His timely intervention probably helped save my life. Without hesitation, Mike and I left before the host could change his mind.

Even though my life had just been threatened, I could not have been more unconcerned. For I felt safely harbored in God's presence as I jumped into my pickup with Mike. Driving down the mountain road, I glanced over at him; silent, he appeared bewildered. I presumed he was troubled about how the host could have followed through on his death threat and included Mike. Instead, Mike finally broke his silence to discuss the surprise supernatural guest who had crashed the party. Mike expressed that he had never seen or experienced anything like this in his life. He sought to understand and wanted answers. Even though I did not understand all that had transpired, I was delighted as I realized that Mike's interest revealed that God was still tugging at his heart. Meanwhile, I remained enraptured in God's majestic glory.

Suddenly, something else profound happened that I had never experienced. A thought raced through my mind, *What am I doing?* Surprisingly, I began speaking in an unknown language. At the time, I did not know what this phenomenon, called speaking in tongues, was. However, I recalled one occasion when I was about twelve while living on the northern Minnesota farmstead. While walking upstairs to speak with my mother, I overheard her praying yet couldn't understand what she was saying. Because the sound was so foreign, it remained etched in my memory.

> *Follow the way of love and eagerly desire gifts of the Spirit. For anyone who speaks in a tongue does not speak to people but to God. Indeed, no one understands them; they utter mysteries by the Spirit. Anyone who speaks in a tongue edifies themselves. I would like every one of you to speak in tongues.*
>
> — *1 Corinthians 14:1a, 2, 4a, 5a*

I now realize that my mother had been speaking in tongues, otherwise referred to as a personal prayer language.

On our drive back to St. Regis I could tell that having been exposed to my speaking in tongues was too much for Mike. The poor guy became frightened and frantically reached for the door handle to jump out of the truck. The only problem was that Mike and I were traveling down the road at fifty-five miles per hour. To prevent him from jumping to his possible death, I told him I would stop. After Mike regained his composure, I regretted my insensitivity for overwhelming him.

Arriving in St. Regis, God spoke to my heart. He had one more mission for me to accomplish before the night was over, and I was eager to comply. Nearing the home of Bo, the witch, I informed Mike that I intended to stop by to share with her about the night's events. Inviting him to join me, I saw him turn pale; Mike looked as though he had seen a ghost.

Mike knew, as did everyone else in our circle of friends, that Bo was an intimidating figure. She would be the last person on earth that he would approach to share anything related to God. Mike vehemently attempted to convince me that my crazy venture was not only foolish but treacherous. He was so upset that he insisted I let him out of the truck when we pulled up to Bo's house. However, Mike requested that I come over the next day to continue our discussion about what had happened at the cocaine party. He needed reassurance that what had transpired was a supernatural encounter with God. I strongly felt it was my mission to dispel the notion that Mike had been subjected to some sort of drug-induced illusion. He also expressed a keen interest in the outcome of my encounter with Bo. I was confident that God was not finished working through Mike's doubt and resistance and savored the opportunity to speak with him the next day. However, foremost on my mind was the risk involved with making a very late-night visit with Bo, the witch.

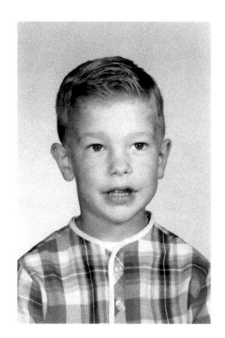

David, 5 years old

David and Roy, 6 and 4 years old

Roy on Corn Cob Hill at Hap and Pearl's Farm

David's mother, Susan

Grandparents Hap and Pearl

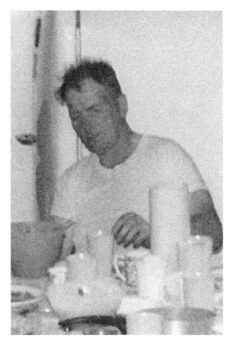

Stepfather Dale

Dale on 706 tractor by The Barn

David and Roy (in cab) on fishing vacation

David, age 10, with his new calf

David's Marine Basic Training portrait

David and Roy with Mom

Tunisian girl at my Marine Corp encampment

David with his trophy bull elk, age 18.

David and Julie on their wedding day

David praying for soldier in airport

My brother, Roy

CHAPTER 9
A Witch's Transformation

When I pulled my truck up to Bo's house, it was about 2:00 a.m. Mike's passenger door had already slammed shut before I could come to a complete stop. As he bolted down the dimly lit street, I remembered that Bo owned a vicious German shepherd named Max. A "Beware of Dog" sign was posted on the front gate. This warning was to be taken seriously.

As the morning hours soon approached, beams of moonlight began piercing through overcast skies giving way to a cold clear night. I reconsidered if stopping by Bo's house was a wise decision and started to second-guess my intentions. Even if I were to miraculously escape a vicious dog attack, would I be any safer sharing God's love with a witch, especially after waking her up in the middle of the night? So I asked God, "Are You with me?" Speaking to my heart, He replied, *"Yes, I am."* Swinging open Bo's front gate further alerted Max. True to his temperament and training, he focused his attention on me like a laser beam, growling louder with every step of my approach. Again, I asked God, "Are You still with me?" His reassuring reply was, *"Yes,"* which was becoming easier to believe. I was amazed that the dog had not already charged me.

Halfway down the sidewalk, I considered it odd that Max seemed to refocus his laser-like attention on something behind me. At that moment, I distinctly felt I was attended by a large and powerful angel. Max's stance seemed to confirm my senses, as his temperament suddenly shifted; he became uncharacteristically submissive. Approaching Bo's dog, I did something I had never dared to do before, even with his owner present. I confidently reached out and patted Max on the head. Surprisingly, he cowered, whimpering under my touch.

Nudging Max out of the way, I knocked on Bo's front door. Waiting for a response gave me one final opportunity to scrub this mission. My plan was taking me into uncharted spiritual territory, where I intended to introduce a witch to God. My apprehension intensified as I was unable to shake off the concern of waking up Bo at such a late hour. Questions began bombarding my mind: *What was I going to say? How was my late-night visit going to be perceived? How would God move in this situation?* My skin tingled as I contemplated uncertain outcomes with only one conclusion remaining. This was going to be a dramatic event. Along with these thoughts, curiosity overcame any insecurity I had. The suspense kept my feet planted.

Draped inside Bo's front door window were sheer lace curtains that allowed me to peer into her living room. Beams of moonlight faintly lit the floor and walls to allow the view of a woman's silhouette walking toward me wearing what looked like a bathrobe. It seemed strange that Bo didn't concern herself with turning on any lights as she came to the door. Instead of opening it, she slowly pushed aside the curtains. After I was sure Bo recognized me, she just stood there as if she were a statue, staring back at me with her piercing eyes. The longer she stood frozen, the more uneasy I felt. With my new God-given gift of discernment, I sensed an evil presence was whispering a lie into Bo's ear, warning her she was going to be threatened by something ominous that was about to happen.

With the lights still turned off, Bo finally opened the door to let me in. Palpably irritated, she asked, "What are you doing here?" I began telling Bo about the cocaine party that I had just left. Because of her connections, she had known about the party, which amplified her irritation for not having been invited. As I began to offer an explanation, Bo abruptly interrupted, "Are you high on coke?" I replied, "No," telling her that I was much higher on something else. Her curiosity aroused, Bo allowed me to continue. Pausing to take a deep breath, I knew it was time to get straight to the point. I said, "Jesus just saved me, and I am never going to be the same again!" Once again, with God's gift of discernment, I could see through Bo's piercing eyes into a soul that was totally enslaved by demonic possession. The evil spirit that had taken up residence in her soul needed to be shown who was boss and kicked out through God's power. Meanwhile, I sensed a little girl trapped inside her soul desperately crying out, "*Let me out! Let me go!*" Seeing Bo's imprisonment, I told her, "You can have Jesus, too. He can set you free!"

With battle lines drawn, a raging war was about to begin in the ranks of the spiritual realm over the possession of Bo's soul. Something had to give way as God's liberating power descended upon this dark arts practitioner and His love began to embrace her. Without my speaking another word, suddenly, Bo fell to her knees and began wailing in extreme agony. Poisonous toxins from deep within her soul bubbled up, oozing from her septic spiritual wounds. The supernatural surgery being performed before my very eyes, albeit ugly and unruly, was turning out to be the most precious and beautiful event I had ever witnessed. I silently observed Bo as she allowed God's presence to continue to work on cleansing her.

After witnessing Bo's powerful deliverance, she started to settle and softly weep. Finally, she was able to speak. After she sorrowfully confessed the evil that she had committed against God and others, I asked Bo if she wanted to give her life to Jesus. She humbly whispered, "Yes." Bo was physically drained by this experience, so I helped her up and escorted her across the living room. Sitting her down, I knelt beside her in the dimly lit room. Reaching out, I took hold of Bo's hands to lead her in prayer. As she continued gently weeping, in that sacred moment, Bo asked God to forgive her, to cleanse her, to take up residence in her heart, and to be the new Lord of her life. "If we confess our sins, He is faithful and just and will forgive us our sins and purify us from all unrighteousness" (1 John 1:9). "For He [God] has rescued us from the dominion of darkness and brought us into the kingdom of the Son He loves" (Colossians 1:13). As the dark of night surrendered to the dawn of a new morning, Bo was rescued from an eternal destiny in Hell and given a forever heavenly home in God's kingdom.

Hopping into my truck and leaving Bo's dramatic transformation behind, I returned home with tears sown in gratitude toward God. Humbled, I reflected on my life-changing New Year's Eve whirlwind experience. God chose this unforgettable night to reintroduce Himself to me in His glory and power; along with others, I was forever transformed.

Back home, I awoke late the next morning still enveloped in the overwhelmingly loving presence of God. After a quick shower and breakfast, I hightailed it over to Mike's place to confirm that the prior evening's encounter with God was not the result of a drug-induced delusion. Before we talked, he was already convinced that this event was real and came from God. No one could have been subjected to such a powerful display of God's life-changing power and believed otherwise. Tears flowed as I conveyed to Mike how Bo surrendered her life to God. His presence came upon Mike as I affirmed God's love for him. Suddenly, Mike's wall of resistance finally came crashing down; he wept. Then he shared how he had feared entering into uncharted waters where God would take over as captain of his ship. Overcoming his fear, Mike expressed his need to finally make things right with God. I offered to pray with him to accept Jesus into his heart. "For God so loved the world that He gave His one and only Son, that whoever believes in Him shall not perish but have eternal life" (John 3:16). Before I left, Mike revealed that his parents had been praying for him for a long time and that he intended to call them immediately. Following my conversation with Mike that morning, I felt the urgency to leave Montana along with its danger and snares and return home to Minnesota. However, I was about to run into my worst enemy, a gun-toting Mafia member.

CHAPTER 10
Mafia Meetup

God impressed upon me to call my mother in Minnesota. We wept as I shared my life-changing divine encounter, and her heart overflowed with tears of joy. Asking my mother if I could return home to reconcile our once close relationship would help fulfill a new spiritual priority. Growing up, I was well aware of her intimate relationship with God and how she always kept her Bible close. Transparent and vocal about her faith, my mother once dared to share Christ with Dale early in their marriage. I had many conversations with her about God before she met him. Especially memorable was one talk my mother and I had when I was just six years old. I expressed to her that Jesus would rapture His followers and take them to Heaven during her lifetime.

For the Lord Himself will come down from Heaven,
with a loud command, with the voice of the archangel
and with the trumpet call of God, and the dead in
Christ will rise first. After that, we who are still alive
and are left will be caught up with them in the clouds

to meet the Lord in the air. And so we will be with
the Lord forever.

— 1 Thessalonians 4:16–17

Rather than dismissing my view of Christ's return to the earth for His church, she found my prediction interesting. Because of her well-seasoned faith, I knew my mother would be delighted to mentor me in the wisdom and ways of God.

Several days later, I boarded a flight home with all the possessions I owned stuffed into a couple of seabags. I was bound for a new life with God as my author, writing another adventurous chapter in my story. Leaving St. Regis, Montana, the mission of sharing God's love with Mike, Bo, and Thumper had ended. Now it was my hope and prayer that God would bring others into their lives to water the seeds which I had planted. "I planted the seed, Apollos watered it, but God made it grow" (1 Corinthians 3:6).

Aboard my flight from Missoula, Montana, to Sioux Falls, South Dakota, I had ample time to tell other passengers on the plane of my recent supernatural encounter. I had the pleasure of sharing with them about an incredibly powerful, faithful, and loving God. Before touching down on the wintery tarmac, I was not the only one on the plane who had tears streaming down their face.

During the flight, I also reflected on how much I loved and appreciated my mother after subjecting her to the burden of my troubled teenage years. Surviving Dale's POW camp had taken a substantial emotional and spiritual toll on my life. After my mother divorced him and returned to southern Minnesota, I was shuttled between my father and mother. During this time, the dark forces of hatred and bitterness continued to attempt to unravel the good work God had done in my heart at age eight. While I stayed with my mother, she depended on me for emotional support to help raise her boys that I felt only a father should provide. However, love and acceptance had been ripped away by both of my fathers. This formed a negative perception of myself as well as my perception of a father's role. Therefore, trying to fulfill this awkward position with my mother felt embarrassing. Instead of helping her, I disengaged, causing her an enormous amount of grief.

When I was fifteen, I purchased a brand new Kawasaki Kz1000 motorcycle, which, at the time, was the fastest production bike on the planet. Speeding around blind corners at over one hundred and twenty miles per hour, it was miraculous that I survived. After receiving five speeding tickets within the first month, my insurance was revoked. Then I returned the motorcycle to the cycle shop owner, who, of course, was very displeased.

Besides racking up speeding tickets, I partnered in crime with a Winnebago High School classmate named Charlie. We committed acts of vandalism and petty theft. One night, Charlie and I took a joyride with his vehicle, tearing up the turf on the local golf course. Our crime spree came to an abrupt halt after we were charged with grand theft auto for stealing a two-ton public utility truck. Before blowing up the engine on our joyride in the countryside, Charlie and I drove up and down the main street. This is when my brother, Roy, saw me with my head hanging out the passenger window as he was headed out of town in the opposite direction driving another stolen car! Roy was never caught for taking numerous unauthorized joyrides, but this ride came to a sudden end when he rolled his stolen car into a ditch.

The darkness in my heart intensified. One day the following summer at age sixteen, I was driving with my mother in her Camaro. Approaching a sharp twenty-five miles per hour corner, I suddenly felt a demonic presence come over me with a powerful urge to end her life and mine. Struggling with this impulse, I slammed the gas pedal to the floor intending to crash into a grove of oak trees just beyond the tight corner. But, by the grace of God, thankfully, I returned to my senses and applied the brakes just in time to avert a tragedy.

Another painful memory involved a time when I pushed my mother down while having a heated argument with her. Sleeping over at my cousin's place the following evening, I awoke the next morning to banging on the door. My father called me outside and delivered a series of cage-rattling blows. I did not defend myself, as I realized that a forbidden line had been crossed with my mother.

During my flight, it humbled me to reflect on how I had caused my mother so many heartaches. Yet I knew all was forgiven. God reaffirmed His forgiveness by setting up a memorable experience between my mother and me after I disembarked from the plane at the Sioux Falls airport.

In the terminal, I was surrounded by a densely packed crowd of several hundred people. Unable to spot my mother, I asked God to help me find her. Then my eyes were directed over to her standing at the far end of the crowd, a considerable distance away. As my mother and I spotted each other, God gave me a glimpse into His spiritual realm so that I could see her through His eyes. I beheld a beautiful and precious woman both inside and out. She was wearing a bright red overcoat with a long black scarf flung over her shoulder. My mother's striking features were highlighted with streaks of white flowing through her jet-black hair. My mother's charm was accentuated with a captivating smile. Remarkably, God allowed me to see her like He saw all of His saints. For a moment, I saw a halo that crowned my lovely mother, and she glistened with a radiant countenance. She glowed like Moses after he saw the burning bush as depicted in the movie *The Ten Commandments*. It seemed the crowd sensed a special moment unfolding as a silence hushed over them, and they parted like the Red Sea. They watched as my mother and I walked toward each other while weeping and then joined in a loving embrace. Kissing her cheek, I wanted everyone to know that she was my mother. For several days, which felt like weeks, I had eagerly anticipated finally telling her in person how much I loved and appreciated her.

The first week I was at home, my mother invited me to meet her pastor. Her church was in the larger neighboring town of Blue Earth, Minnesota. Pastor Miller was standing near the pulpit when he saw me enter the sanctuary. Sizing him up, he was a large man about six feet two and three hundred pounds. Wearing a black leather jacket, Pastor Miller appeared as if he had just returned from a biker's rally. He looked like a half-Japanese sumo wrestler with jet black hair and a "Nacho Libre" mustache who could body slam anyone who got in his way.

I had been informed that Pastor Miller was the son of a Japanese mother and a career military father. It became apparent that his demeanor did not conform to the typical profile of a kind and gentle pastor as he approached me with a booming baritone voice, "I heard about you!" without even the hint of a smile. It appeared as though I was about to be confronted by a potentially dangerous individual. Tactical options from my former military training instinctively began to run through my mind. Concern for my personal safety seemed warranted as Pastor Miller aggressively grabbed me while commanding me, "Bring it on in!" Possessing sumo wrestler-like strength, he hugged me with a force that nearly collapsed my lungs. After the pastor released me, he looked into my eyes while cracking a disarming smile with tears streaming down his cheeks. Seeing this large man weeping and feeling such love coming from his heart profoundly touched me. It was an unforgettable experience that brought tears to my eyes.

My mother's spiritual battle plan to retrieve her long-lost prodigal son was finally successful. She had recruited her church congregation to engage in an organized 24/7 prayer effort for me. Many members, both young and old alike, had participated. Powerful and seasoned prayer warriors spearheaded a special ops prayer chain through her women's fellowship group. No one, not even a Marine, could have survived a targeted strategy of this magnitude without being spiritually impacted for good.

The first week I was back home from Montana, I felt compelled to write Lisa, my former girlfriend, to share about my encounter with God and how I had given my life to Jesus. In my letter, I also expressed regret for how I had lived in sin while dating her and asked Lisa for forgiveness.

Planted at my mother's feet for the next nine months, I grew spiritually from watching her pour out the loving overflow of her relationship with God toward others. I also increased in knowledge from her wise teaching of the Bible. During this time, I experienced several supernatural manifestations. Upon waking each morning, I couldn't wait to read my new Bible with my name embossed in gold letters on the bottom of the front cover. When I opened my Bible for the first few months, I was welcomed with a pleasant fragrance which came from Heaven that would lift off the pages, saturating my senses. Along with developing a deeper scriptural understanding, there were times I received powerful insights that were life-changing revelations. "All Scripture is God-breathed and is useful for teaching, rebuking, correcting and training in righteousness" (2 Timothy 3:16). "For the word of God is alive and active. Sharper than any double-edged sword, it penetrates even to dividing soul and spirit, joints and marrow; it judges the thoughts and attitudes of the heart" (Hebrews 4:12). This is the same Bible that I have kept to this day. Personalizing my Bible helped it become my most treasured possession. I have written copious notes, highlighted multitudinous verses, and wept over its pages as I have grown in faith and character. The rare instance I misplaced it nearly caused panic. Like my dearly beloved wife, Jules, this Bible will remain next to me for the rest of my days; and it would be devastating if I were ever to be separated from it.

During this special time I stayed with my mother, I experienced other supernatural events. One evening when I was upstairs in my bedroom, I sensed an ominous presence. Hopping off the bed, I rushed over to the window. I spotted a demonic black-winged human-sized creature dressed in a red vest wearing a black cape. It was about to enter through the window when it saw me. Startled, the demon quickly reversed course, flying away into the darkness of the night. Having sensed that the creature had intended to do spiritual harm, I felt empowered by God's protection.

Praying late one evening after my mother went to bed, I was kneeling in the living room next to her bedroom. Suddenly, I saw arrows tipped with flames of fire flying through the room and entering her cracked bedroom door. I sensed that they were shot by dark forces with the intent to do spiritual harm. As I engaged in prayer, deploying the full armor of God, the arrows ceased flying. The Bible clearly describes the reality of demonic forces and their weaponry while providing instruction for using God's armor warring against evil powers.

> *Finally, be strong in the Lord and in His mighty power. Put on the full armor of God, so that you can take your stand against the devil's schemes. For our struggle is not against flesh and blood, but against the rulers, against the authorities, against the powers of this dark world and against the spiritual forces of evil in the heavenly realms. In addition to all this, take up the shield of faith, with which you can extinguish all the flaming arrows of the evil one. With this in mind, be alert and always keep on praying for all the Lord's people.*
>
> *— Ephesians 6:10–12, 16, 18b*

It was also during this time, when I was home with my mother, that I received news about Dave, a former Winnebago,

Minnesota, high school classmate. The history between us had been hostile. By the time we were seniors, Dave was a principal drug supplier in our hometown. However, doing drugs wasn't my thing. Even though it was a town of only 1,700 residents, it had gained notoriety for drug trafficking. Winnebago was even dubbed "Little Chicago" and featured on a nationally televised segment of *60 Minutes*.

Dave was an out-of-control class clown who pulled off outlandish pranks on everyone. A dignified event such as our high school graduation ceremony should have been an occasion to exercise self-control. For Dave, however, this was not the case, especially when his misbehavior was fueled by drugs and alcohol. As our class was lining up in the hallway robed in our graduation gowns, he began showing off, verbally jabbing me and wanting to fight. Because I was the strongest student in school and temperamental, everyone knew that messing with me was a foolish idea. Even though Dave was a tough farm kid and an accomplished wrestler, I could have easily become uncaged like a wounded animal and beaten him unconscious. A quickly evolving volatile situation was diffused when the cue to walk out onto the stage was given.

Years later, Dave returned home to Winnebago just months before me. Amazingly, God had dramatically and miraculously transformed his life like mine. No sooner than I had heard the news about his conversion, I was knocking on Dave's door, where he lived on a large crop and hog farm. It was less than two miles from the small rented farm where I had been staying with my mother. As I arrived, a winter day had just given way to a crisp young night sky. As Dave opened the door, a kindred spirit instantly connected us. We embraced each other with a heartfelt hug before a word was even spoken.

Then Dave and I enthusiastically shared our transformative experiences with each other. I told him that God had directed me to return home to begin a new Spirit-led journey. Likewise, Dave told me about his life as a high-level gun-toting Mafia member running drug shipments from Chicago to Winnebago. Eventually, the inherent risks associated with his position as a drug dealer caught up with him. Dave had feared for his life after receiving death threats from other dangerous groups seeking to take over his territory. Seeing the handwriting on the wall, Dave prayed to be rescued. Thankfully, God faithfully answered, turning his life around. Giving his life to God, Dave established his own *Youth for Christ* radio broadcast ministry that reached out to southern Minnesota and northern Iowa. After sharing our stories with each other, we were awed by the grace and mercy of God. His plan was teaming us together to shake up things in our region. Yet neither Dave nor I could have imagined that an even greater adventure was about to begin.

CHAPTER 11

Gangsters on Fire

The following Sunday, after reconnecting with Dave, my new spiritual brother, I attended church with him, my mother, and my three stepbrothers. The service had barely begun when Pastor Miller unexpectedly deviated from his prepared message and opened up the pulpit for anyone who wanted to share their testimony. God was tugging at my heartstrings, and I felt the need to share my life-changing experience. As I stood up, Pastor Miller gave me a nod to come forward. Making my way to the pulpit, I found myself in a similar situation as I had at the New Year's Eve cocaine party when I had wondered what I was going to say. Standing at the mic, I looked out over the sanctuary; and tears began to flow. Several moments later, all I could manage to say through tears was, "Jesus just saved me, and I am never going to be the same again." Looking up, I saw the pastor and congregation weeping. The preplanned service had ended as soon as it had begun with God's Spirit spontaneously moving, which prompted an eruption of shared collective praise.

Following the service, I was inundated with hugs from people whom I had never met. One little boy, who was about five years old, was tugging at my pant leg; so I knelt down to look him in the eyes. With tears streaming down his cheeks, he told me in his innocent little voice that he and his family had been praying for me every night before they went to bed. My heart melted; I was undone.

Consumed with God's business, Dave and I were on fire. We kicked off a single adults' Bible study and prayer group. The meeting was hosted on a rotational basis between Dave's place and my mother's house. In addition, Dave and I attended Sunday morning and evening services along with Wednesday night fellowship meetings. Our hunger to be in God's alluring presence and in the joyful fellowship of other believers was insatiable.

God moved powerfully. Within a short time, our home meetings consistently went longer than planned. Our one evening per week gathering rapidly grew to meeting every night, expanding to include married couples. With our homes running out of space, the overflow of our growing group flooded the main church services, dramatically increasing church attendance. Throughout the region, news spread like wildfire that many people were being brought to a saving knowledge of Jesus Christ. In addition, others were receiving supernatural physical healings or were being delivered from their addictions. For some, it was like the circus had come to town, and curiosity drew them; others came with personal and spiritual needs. "Believe in the Lord Jesus, and you will be saved—you and your household" (Acts 16:31b). "So if the Son sets you free, you will be free indeed" (John 8:36). Regardless, attendance exploded; and we found ourselves in the midst of a spiritual revival.

If there was any spare time, the core of our singles' group, Dave, Rick and Kim, Lynette, DJ, and I, met together, making many cherished memories. Rolling into a Godfather's Pizza or McDonald's in a neighboring town such as Fairmont or Blue Earth, Minnesota, our group was overflowing with the love of God. Individuals and small groups were drawn to our abundant joy and contagious laughter, so they were eager to come join us. Many asked for prayer, and some accepted Christ as their Savior. Sharing the Good News of the Gospel on the proverbial highways, byways, and street corners was our greatest pleasure. "The Spirit of the Lord is on me, because He has anointed me to proclaim good news to the poor. He has sent me to proclaim freedom for the prisoners and recovery of sight for the blind, to set the oppressed free, to proclaim the year of the Lord's favor" (Luke 4:18–19). Hearing about our adventures and how they impacted our region, Pastor Miller nicknamed our group the "Gospel Gangsters."

Even with a revival fire burning in our region, practical matters, including earning an income and helping my mother put food on the table, were pressing responsibilities. DJ, a member of our Gospel Gangsters group, and I worked together during the following summer. We were hired by a construction company to erect nine galvanized steel grain bins that were several stories tall. The building site was on the outskirts of the small town of Huntley, Minnesota, where I had previously lived as a five-year-old. The job was physically demanding. Heavy four-by-eight-foot sheets of one-quarter-inch thick-ribbed steel had to be maneuvered into place, where they were stacked and bolted down by hand. The four-man crew that we joined was a surly and salty bunch that would even make a pirate blush. They were led by John, the crew's fearless and immoral foreman. He was short and scruffy with a beer belly and prickly whiskers. Faded tattoos on John's wrinkled arms stretched beyond their original shapes and were indecipherable from years of toil under the sun. His gruff chainsaw-sounding voice gave away that he was a chronic smoker. Even though John looked to be in his late thirties, his appearance told the story of someone who had already lived a hard life. The other three men on the crew were younger than John yet older than DJ and me. Sharp words spoken by each of the crew members pierced the air with expletives containing God's and Jesus' names taken in vain. Conversations were often corrupted with vile and sexually explicit subject matter. The crew's attitude toward us made it clear that DJ and I could not be accepted into their social circle.

After the first day on the job, I was burdened for the crew. I felt God's love for them and that He wanted me to introduce them to His Son, Jesus, but through my actions alone. This strategy would require daily prayer so God could begin to open the hearts of the crew members and give me the strength to persevere. Sharing my plan with DJ, he agreed to participate. Unlike DJ, who was more reserved, living by example without using words would be more challenging for me, as I was very outgoing. However, successfully representing God through actions alone would provide the opportunity to share the love of God with the crew verbally.

From the beginning, DJ and I were despised by the work crew. Nonetheless, we launched our working relationship with them demonstrating unconditional acts of respect and kindness. Without speaking about God, "Operation Live by Example" began. It wasn't easy. Countless times each day, someone would blurt out a crude joke or mimic vile behavior that kicked off a competition. The first to either provoke indignation or be rewarded with an encouraging chuckle from either DJ or myself would be highly praised. This would jeopardize our plan. Instead, we refused to compromise our standing with our "Operation Live by Example" mission. With prayer and by His grace, DJ and I were able to demonstrate God's love because, "Love is patient, love is kind. It is not easily angered. Love does not delight in evil" (1 Corinthians 13:4a, 5b, 6a).

At times, it was tempting to give in just a little and smile or laugh to show the crew members that DJ and I were also human. Nevertheless, with God's help, we exercised restraint, staying the course. However, our effort fed a growing awkwardness and tension, which created an increasingly difficult spiritual test. I sensed that the crew was watching DJ's and my every move. If we could be tripped up, our representation of God would be sullied, and our positive influence lost. With the eternal destiny of souls at risk, the stakes could not have been higher. Thankfully, God's convicting power became evident when there was a noticeable decrease in the crew's obscene language and behavior.

As our grain bin construction project was nearing an end, one final Friday our crew was standing around at noon with nothing to do. The last load of steel to complete the job had been unexpectedly held up an hour's drive away in northern Iowa. John, the foreman, made the decision that it would be more expeditious to pick up the load ourselves. This provided a valid excuse to take a long and welcome break. At the time, I was unaware that there was a divinely orchestrated plan in the making when everyone piled into John's work van. Sardined into one vehicle for an extended period of time amplified the uneasiness between the crew and DJ and me. A deafening silence held us all hostage. One of the guys would inject some small talk in an attempt to ease the smothering effect of the silence in the crowded van. Returning to the jobsite with the load of steel, we felt the tension build after DJ and I graciously declined to join in chugging down a case of beer with the rest of the crew. John decided to drink rather than drive and had no concern that the driver was doing both. The crew's top priority was to get primed for another weekend of heavy drinking. A Friday afternoon before a beer-drinking weekend would have normally put John in a good mood. Instead, he had a sober look on his face. As I noticed John's demeanor, I pondered if God was dealing with his heart.

After working with the crew for three months, the moment that DJ and I had been hoping and praying for finally arrived. Turning around and breaking through the deafening silence, John asked me what it was that made me different. Recognizing my cue and eager to reply, I noticed that the rest of the crew was also listening intently. My answer was the few but same eternally significant words that I had spoken before, "Jesus saved me; and you can have Him, too." John, having witnessed DJ's and my unwavering characters, now had witnessed our integrity such that these words could positively impact his heart. "Operation Live by Example," which God had helped DJ and I execute, although tested through trying times, had been well worth the effort.

John then asked if I could pray for him, and the rest of the crew wanted me to pray for them as well. Following my lead, they reverently removed their baseball caps, bowing their heads to pray. Afterward, John told me that this was the first time he had ever prayed to God. He expressed how dissatisfied he was with his life. Therefore, he felt that he had nothing to lose in further considering a decision to give his life to God. Fulfilling the job of sharing God's love through actions, DJ and I parted ways with the crew, never to see them again. Yet, we left them with a new life-changing path to follow.

That same summer God strongly moved on my heart again, prompting me to intercede for Dale, my former stepfather. Up until my life-changing experience, I was consumed with exacting revenge by taking his life. However, while praying, God poured out His love upon me for Dale. The floodgate of my heart opened like a dam, releasing pressure from a river of hatred and anger that had raged in the barn. After finally forgiving Dale, my affliction was washed away. It was as if a peaceful meadow along still waters was waiting to refresh my weary soul. Tearfully, I pleaded with God to spare Dale from being taken into eternal darkness. I knew that my heart was healed when surprisingly a strong desire emerged to see him again. I asked God to provide an opportunity to invite Dale over for a cup of coffee to extend love and forgiveness toward him. I had planned to earnestly seek his forgiveness for threatening his life in my mother's kitchen.

However, reconnecting with Dale never happened. After my mother divorced him, he sold the northern Minnesota farm and relocated to Missouri. Dale remarried a reportedly wicked woman before his death many years later. She took him for everything, including a vast sum of money and the inheritance of his three biological sons. Dale's life painfully ended when he suffered from a violent internal rupture. Yet, my hope remains that sometime after the barn, Dale accepted Christ as his Savior. For "people are destined to die once, and after that to face judgment" (Hebrews 9:27b).

> *Then I saw a great white throne and Him [God] who was seated on it. And I saw the dead, great and small, standing before the throne, and books were opened. Another book was opened, which is the book of life. The dead were judged according to what they had done as recorded in the books. Anyone whose name was not found written in the book of life was thrown into the lake of fire.*
>
> — *Revelation 20:11a, 12, 15*

One unforgettable day later that summer, Pastor Miller invited Dave and me to join him in attending an upcoming statewide Minnesota pastors' conference in Minneapolis. The invitation struck me as curious since we weren't pastors. Nonetheless, Dave and I accepted. I considered it a privilege to attend the conference.

There were about 1,000 pastors gathered in a mega-church-sized building. I had never seen such a large and beautiful auditorium. In addition to the statewide pastoral leadership, the Minnesota superintendent overseeing all the denomination's pastors in the state was in attendance and speaking from a gigantic platform. Seated with Pastor Miller and Dave, I soaked in the magnificence of my surroundings. It was then that the speaker diverted from the beginning of his prepared message and unexpectedly became silent. I sensed that something extraordinary was about to happen. *Hold it... would God want me to share my testimony here?* Struggling with this notion, I felt my heart race as God prompted me to share my supernatural encounter with those in attendance. While the speaker appeared to be engaged in silent prayer, I stood and walked out into a center aisle. Apprehension challenged each step I made on my way up to the platform. *Was I committing an egregious act? Was I going to be humbled by being told to sit back down? Why couldn't the speaker just look up and give me a nod like Pastor Miller had done before?* It felt as though my heart was going to pound out of my chest. Yet I continued trusting that each step I took by faith was led by God.

As I stepped up onto the platform, the speaker lifted his head and glanced at me. Without hesitation, he yielded the plexiglass pulpit as I approached. There I was, standing at a mic once again. I began to tell the story about my transformational encounter with God. With tears streaming down my cheeks, I felt God's presence rest upon me in a special way. I ended my testimony with these familiar words, "Jesus saved me, and I am never going to be the same again!" Once more, a prepared service had ended as soon as it had begun as 1,000 pastors were caught up in heartfelt Spirit-led weeping and sponta-neous, joyful praise. As incredible as this experience was, God was about to reveal to me that all things are indeed possible. "Jesus looked at them and said, 'With man this is impossible, but with God all things are possible'" (Matthew 19:26). God was about to fulfill a dream that I had.

CHAPTER 12
Beyond the Barn

Throughout the time that I had the pleasure of staying with my mother in Winnebago, Minnesota, I was consumed with developing a deeper relationship with God and understanding the Bible. One source of inspiration was the Trinity Broadcasting Network on television. I watched well-known pastors, evangelists, and teachers as they conveyed inspirational messages and expounded upon biblical principles. One notable broadcast was the *A Study in the Word* program hosted by evangelist Jimmy Swaggart. His television ministry was viewed by millions of people worldwide. I was also positively influenced by one of Swaggart's regular panelists, Reverend Charles Worthington. During weekly programming, he taught an uncompromising Christian worldview reinforced with straightforward and insightful biblically-based teaching. Furthermore, Charles Worthington was a highly regarded Bible professor. He taught at the then prestigious Jimmy Swaggart Bible College (JSBC) in Baton Rouge, Louisiana. I had hoped that one day I would be able to enroll at JSBC and attend Professor Worthington's classes.

My prayers were answered in a way that exceeded my wildest dreams and in a place I least expected. Instead of attending JSBC, I enrolled in Trinity Bible College (TBC) to earn a Bible/Ministerial degree in the fall of 1987. Initially, this remote college campus of only 500 students gave me the impression that it was not the ideal place to go chasing after big dreams. TBC, located in a seemingly insignificant area of the country 50 miles east of somewhere and a 100 miles north of nowhere, was quietly nestled in a small town of about 1,000 residents. From the flat countryside surrounding Ellendale, North Dakota, one could see for miles in any given direction. The few dogs seen ran around nervously where trees were rare. Persistent strong summer winds whipping up over endless fields produced spectacular mystifying dust devils, creating the ideal sagebrush dream. Some of the coldest winters in the nation stung residents' faces with fierce winds and blinding whiteouts. Even so, I selected this school because it was also chosen by DJ, one of the former Gospel Gangsters, and my previous summer grain bin construction partner. The college was also conveniently located only a few hours' drive from my mother's great cooking. Most of all, I was partial to the laid-back, small-town rural setting.

During my sophomore year in 1988, reports came out that shook the Christian world. Jimmy Swaggart Bible College had been ensnared in a scandal involving its founder and evangelist, Jimmy Swaggart. This devastating news crushed me. I was also concerned about how this development would undoubtedly tarnish Christ's name throughout the world and embolden critics of Christianity. Subsequently, many of Jimmy Swaggart Bible College's faculty members and students transferred to other affiliated Bible colleges throughout the nation.

One morning after beginning my junior year at Trinity Bible College, I was having breakfast in the cafeteria when I had a surprise visitor. Seated alone, I was preoccupied with the Swaggart news when I was interrupted by an older distinguished familiar-looking gentleman. Amazingly, it was Reverend Charles Worthington, the professor whom I had dreamed of meeting. To my delight, he asked to join me at my table. My conversation with him was surreal given that I had recently seen him on television along with millions of people worldwide. Professor Worthington and I instantly connected, and a unique bond was established. God had answered my prayer to meet him and even provided me with the opportunity to attend several of his classes. Professor Worthington's son, Joel, had also arrived as a new student. Later Joel would become a close friend and even the best man at my future wedding.

There was also an attractive young woman who arrived on campus with Professor Worthington along with other former JSBC students. The first time I saw Julie was when she was invited up on stage during the initial student body assembly of the year. She was introduced as the student who had traveled the furthest to attend Trinity Bible College. Julie had just flown in from Germany after having visited her mother, whose husband was stationed in the Air Force there. I was eager to meet Julie, being a world traveler myself. On stage, her snappy peach-colored dress was bedazzling. Up close, Julie's sparkling blue eyes and attractive smile, accentuated by a bubbly personality, forever captivated my heart.

I decided to ask Julie for a date. She had no idea what she was getting into, dating a character like me. Our first date at an all-you-can-eat buffet was an eye-opener for her. After finishing our meal, the soft-serve ice cream machine was calling us. Julie watched in disbelief as I loaded an ice cream cone nearly two feet high and begged me to stop. Attracting stares and laughs as we walked back to our table in the crowded restaurant, she was beyond embarrassed. In a way, the cone could have been considered an indication as to what Julie would be getting herself into with dating me.

In 1989, during the summer between my junior and senior years, a college friend of ours invited a group of students, including Julie and me, to work at a fish cannery in our friend's hometown of Cordova, Alaska. At summer's end we flew into Seattle. While waiting for a connecting flight to return to college, I took Julie to the Space Needle for lunch. At the height of over 600 feet, it seemed the perfect place to propose to her. Having survived the ice cream cone incident, Julie and I had grown in our relationship and in sharing a solid faith. It was atop this landmark observation tower that Julie accepted my proposal, and we began planning our future together.

Julie and I were married on October 14, 1989, in Aberdeen, South Dakota. Our wedding, attended by family, friends, faculty members, and fellow students, was officiated by Trinity Bible College president, S. Robert Maddox. Shortly after Julie and I were married, Professor Worthington invited us to join him in living off-campus on his property. We roughed it out in a travel trailer parked next to his residence. During this time, my admiration for Professor Worthington continued to grow. After sharing his biblical knowledge with people worldwide, this renowned man of God invited Julie and me over to his home. Evening after evening, he imparted wisdom to us as we sat next to the fireplace. The personal setting in which this great man of God mentored me far exceeded what I could have ever dreamed. The Bible speaks about how God exceeds our expectations when it says, "Now to Him who is able to do immeasurably more than all we ask or imagine, according to His power that is at work within us, to Him be glory" (Ephesians 3:20–21a).

While attending Trinity Bible College, two years had passed since I had experienced my divine encounter at the New Year's Eve cocaine party with Thumper in 1987. I was surprised one day to meet the widow of one of his co-workers, who was also attending the college, and I was amazed at how God had arranged for us to cross paths. Her husband had recently died while working with Thumper on a high-voltage transmission tower. After describing the experience that I had with Thumper, she provided me with his phone number; and I called him. Although our conversation was brief, he expressed how unforgettable our supernatural encounter had been with God. I sensed that Thumper was forever changed by the experience.

After I received my Bible/Ministerial BA degree and Julie earned her Office Administration AA degree, in 1989, we moved to Arlington, Washington. My intention had been to pursue a master's degree in theology from Regent University in British Columbia with the ultimate goal of obtaining a doctorate degree. But God had different plans for me. "In his heart a man plans his course, but the Lord determines his steps" (Proverbs 16:9). Instead, I helped advance the kingdom of God as a workingman's evangelist. God placed me in various blue-collar jobs where I was able to share His love and lead people to salvation in Christ. Julie and I were also involved in several Christian ministries, including teaching children, pastoring at a nursing home, and leading worship at church while we were working at various jobs. Even so, there were many occasions when I felt I had somehow missed my calling to full-time ministry. Perceiving myself to be a failure, God would remind me that wherever He sent me, individuals were influenced for His glory through a saving knowledge of Jesus Christ.

By 1998, Julie and I had moved from Arlington to Mukilteo, Washington; and I started working at Boeing, where she had been employed for several years. While working at the birthplace of the 747 as an electrician at the Everett, Washington, facility, I continued to have the opportunity to share my faith and lead people to Christ. At Boeing there was an influential co-worker in my department whom I will refer to as Mark. As a member of the Wiccan church, he was a broker in the kingdom of darkness. Intelligent and articulate, Mark's powers of persuasion were evident as he engaged other co-workers in passionate philosophical and ideological conversations. While working with him, he made his rounds of discussion with almost everyone. Yet Mark rarely approached me due to the spiritual tension between us. Even though he effectively steered others toward accepting his self-indulgent worldview devoid of spiritual consequence, I sensed his insecurity. Mark still seemed to be searching for absolute truth, including the reason for his existence. As I began praying for him, God gave me a prophetic vision that He was going to intervene in this man's life and place a powerful evangelistic call upon him. In this vision I saw Mark preaching the Word of God to the masses and leading them to Christ. After this, I approached him at work and asked if I could speak to him privately. Mark tearfully responded as I shared God's vision. I asked if I could pray for him, and he gladly accepted. God touched Mark's life that day, and a seed of salvation was sown.

My beautiful wife, Julie, gifted in business administration, gained favor wherever she worked, including at Boeing. She provided guided tours of Boeing's factory, the largest manufacturing facility in the world. There were times when I turned on the television and saw Julie being interviewed on Seattle news stations. She gave guided factory and bus tours to visitors from all over the globe, including private tours that she provided to international dignitaries and world leaders.

My relationship with my brother, Roy, was strained over the ten years following my life-altering encounter with God. After this monumental shift, we found ourselves standing on opposite sides of a spiritual chasm. As I went off to Bible college to follow God's leading, Roy did not seem to understand my calling and remained lost in darkness.

One summer morning a call came in from Roy. At the time, he was a superintendent for Washington Construction, the largest road construction company in the world. Roy supervised sizeable crews that operated heavy equipment to build interstate highways, overpasses, and bridges throughout the Pacific Northwest. I was proud of my brother's accomplishments. Within seven years, Roy quickly climbed his way up to the position of company superintendent. For the purpose of blasting through mountains to build highways, he held a Master Blaster license, which was the highest level certification for civilian use of explosives. Roy was authorized to purchase explosives over the counter. This license also provided authorization for interstate use of explosives on any kind of demolition project regardless of scale in all lower forty-eight states. Even though Roy had the power to blast his way through any mountain, there was a long-standing spiritual mountain in his way that only the almighty God could remove.

Roy had climbed to the pinnacle of success in the road construction world. However, even standing at that summit did not offer him the vantage point he needed to see his way out of a dark place disconnected from God. Roy had always felt cheated, misplaced, and judged as a second-class human being. Cursed and beaten by an evil stepfather, Roy was further misled and felt snubbed for having an immoral biological father. Roy's lifestyle of excessive drinking and fighting even into adulthood was useless in medicating the fierce symptoms of a soul scorched by anger and hatred. Working his high-stress job on the road for at least three weeks out of the month, he was rarely home with his wife and two children. Roy felt that his rough work crew was his family; he got what he deserved. As a superintendent, he worked sixteen-hour days, seven days a week, attempting to drink his troubles away at the local bar until 2 a.m. Roy continued to brawl just like he had as a teenager.

One summer Friday evening in 1993, Roy's crew was working on a road project. The work site was close enough to allow everyone to go back home for the weekend. However, instead of going home to see his wife, son, and daughter, Roy stayed in town to drink with the intention of throwing it all away, including his life. He had not slept for two days, yet drank until dawn. Afterward, he drove up to his vacated jobsite and parked next to a guardrail at the top of Lost Trail Pass. Stepping out of his company truck, Roy looked out over the pass, yelling at the top of his lungs, "I am done with this!" This is when God spoke to his heart and said, "*So am I; here I am.*" At that moment, Roy humbly replied, "I accept You, Lord." A man's man not known for tearing up, he wept. Roy then yelled out at the top of his lungs one more time, "Yahoo!" Before the echo boomeranged off the mountain ridge and returned to his ears, he felt the Holy Spirit swoop in to save him. It was then that Roy knew that he was instantly saved on Lost Trail Pass. From that day forward, Roy's life changed; and he stopped the heavy drinking. As his personal relationship with God grew, he was given the precious opportunity to share his faith with his family. He wept on his knees alongside his son, Buck, followed in time by his daughter, Delray, leading them in a sinner's prayer to accept Christ. Later, Roy's wife, WaNell, joined them and also accepted Jesus as her Savior.

> *"If you declare with your mouth, 'Jesus is Lord,' and believe in your heart that God raised Him from the dead, you will be saved. For it is with your heart that you believe and are justified, and it is with your mouth that you profess your faith and are saved"*
>
> — *Romans 10:9–10*

Thankfully, my prayer was finally answered that Roy and his whole family would be saved.

After those ten long years with almost no relationship with my brother, Roy told me that he had made a commitment to follow Christ and serve Him. Thereafter, Roy and I engaged in frequent phone conversations, many of which centered on the things of God. Foremost among our discussions was the topic of forgiveness, specifically that of forgiving Dale. During our discussion, Roy opened up and shared what was going on in his heart. He admitted his ongoing struggle with unforgiveness and asked how I was able to forgive Dale. "For if you forgive other people when they sin against you, your heavenly Father will also forgive you. But if you do not forgive others their sins, your Father will not forgive your sins" (Matthew 6:14–15). My simple answer to Roy's question was one that I had previously discovered for myself; I encouraged him to start praying for Dale's lost soul. Praying for him would hopefully begin a healing process that would soften Roy's heart, enabling him to forgive Dale. "Be kind and compassionate to one another, forgiving each other, just as in Christ God forgave you" (Ephesians 4:32). My suggestion to Roy was to place himself in a hypothetical scenario. I asked him to imagine something. If Dale were to show up on his doorstep, would he be able to invite him in for a cup of coffee? Roy thought that although my suggestion was simple, he would use it to test his heart. Thankfully, he was eventually able to pass this test in forgiving Dale.

Today Roy and I are the closest of brothers and the best of friends. He, being my brother, not only by blood but also in spirit because of our personal relationships with God, has been one of God's greatest treasures in my life. On many occasions, I have found myself seeking my brother's discerning counsel. I have witnessed him demonstrate Christ's love and forgiveness, especially when being falsely accused or unfairly treated. To this day, Roy remains a steadfast example of excellent character and inspirational faith.

During the time that my relationship with my brother was disconnected, I also prayed for my father's salvation. Many years had passed when one day he called me to share that he had accepted Christ as his Savior. My father told me that after my dramatic conversion, he began to scrutinize how I lived out my commitment to Christ and to my wife, Julie. By the grace of God, the radical and enduring changes I had made compelled my father to give his life to Christ. He also conveyed regret for failing to be a Christ-like example while he raised his family. My father realized how his immoral behavior had corrupted the lives of those closest to him, causing a lingering negative spiritual impact. Asking for forgiveness, he wept. At that moment, it was a great pleasure to assure my father that I had forgiven him long ago and affirm him in God's love. I expressed how thankful I was that he had finally joined me on my journey with Christ. I was overjoyed that now I could ask for my father's prayer support and counsel. "For nothing is impossible with God" (Luke 1:37).

Along with working to advance God's kingdom by winning people to Christ, He also opened doors for me to minister to several national political leaders. In addition, a divine appointment took place with one Army soldier fresh out of Basic Training. On October 5, 2014, I was flying home from a business trip in San Diego, California. While in the Las Vegas, Nevada, terminal waiting for a connecting flight to Spokane, Washington, I noticed a young Army soldier dressed in camouflage fatigues standing alone at a window staring out over the tarmac. Feeling camaraderie toward him as a Marine veteran, I walked over to see how he was doing and give him moral support. After we exchanged introductions, I thanked the young soldier, whose name was Michael, for his service. He explained that he was destined for Spokane to visit his family before heading to his first assigned duty station in Kansas to be a sentry guarding the main gate. With the recent uptick in terrorist activity at military bases, I was concerned for Michael's safety. I was familiar with terrorism, having been deployed to Beirut, Lebanon, in October 1983. Two weeks after frequenting a military installation to socialize, a truck bomb attack took place; 307 lives perished.

During my conversation with Michael, I asked if I could pray for him; and he accepted. So I placed my hand on his shoulder as we both bowed our heads in prayer. After the prayer, I sensed Michael was touched; and I was thankful to have had the honor of praying for him. Unexpectantly, we were interrupted by a personable, attractive blonde-haired woman who was in tears. Unaware of who she was, she told me that her name was Sunny Sweeney and that she had been having a crappy day. She expressed that she was deeply touched watching me pray for Michael, and this gave her hope that there was still some goodness left in this dark world. Sunny asked if it was all right that she had taken a picture of me praying for Michael. She also requested that we exchange phone numbers so she could text the picture to me.

Several days later, my oldest son, Solomon, informed me that the picture of me praying for Michael was posted by Sunny Sweeney, a country music star. My son also told me that the photo had gone viral with over two million hits. Thereafter, friends and acquaintances from all over the country contacted my wife, Julie, on Facebook, offering their congratulations. The post ended up making it into BuzzFeed's Top Viral Sensations for 2014. "Now to Him who is able to do immeasurably more than all we can ask or imagine, according to His power that is at work within us, to Him be glory" (Ephesians 3:20–21a). It is amazing how God can work in such a powerful way when we step out by faith to do even the simplest of things.

The three promises that God audibly spoke to me during that life-altering New Year's Eve cocaine party thirty-five years ago have been fulfilled. First, God's promise of setting me free from drugs and alcohol has remained unshakeable. Secondly, my beautiful wife, whom God had promised, and I affectionately refer to as Jules, has been my faithful companion for over three decades. Our marriage has ripened like a fine wine. Thirdly, as for receiving the promise of a successful life, I am the father of four sons, Solomon, Gabriel, Isaiah, and Seth, each with God-given gifts and on their way to becoming men of God. I have had numerous opportunities to share God's love and mighty life-changing power wherever I go, which is just as exciting to me now as it was then.

My story would not have been possible if it had not been for my mother's diligent intercession for me, which moved the heart of God. She never gave up praying for me, even when I was hopelessly unable to climb out of the deepest pit I had ever dug. By faith, my mother knew it was then I would begin grasping for a lifeline. God knew that I would begin to "reach up" to where He could "reach down" to rescue me in the midst of my darkness. "The prayer of a righteous person is powerful and effective" (James 5:16b). God had spoken to my heart during that unforgettable cocaine party years ago to confirm that He had rescued me because of my mother's prayers.

Looking back over the story of my life, I am no longer regretful but instead thankful that God brought me into this world. In spite of the atrocities and trauma I suffered in the barn, I no longer believe the lie that I am unloved. His limitless love and faithfulness have freed me, transforming me into a new man. "Therefore, if anyone is in Christ, he is a new creation; the old has gone, the new has come" (2 Corinthians 5:17). In my personal relationship with my Heavenly Father, He speaks to my heart and is delighted to tell me in many ways that I am His beloved son. "In love He [our Heavenly Father] predestined us to be adopted as His children through Jesus Christ, in accordance with His pleasure and will" (Ephesians 1:4c, 5). My Heavenly Father's love has healed me so that I can accept who I am and unconditionally love others.

Finally, it has been a distinct honor and pleasure to have had this opportunity to share my personal testimony of God's transformational power. He desires for you to receive His boundless love and blessings by inviting Jesus Christ into your heart. "Here I am! I stand at the door and knock. If anyone hears My voice and opens the door, I will come in and eat with that person, and they with Me" (Revelation 3:20). It is my prayer that you will also experience the peace and wonder of a personal and loving relationship with the living God.

AFTERWORD
What's in Your Future?

It would be my great pleasure and honor to help you make the most important decision in your life, one that will determine your eternal destiny. "People are destined to die once, and after that to face judgment" (Hebrews 9:27b). If you desire to accept Christ, here are some important things to consider.

In truth, the sobering reality is that "all have sinned and fall short of the glory of God" (Romans 3:23). We are all separated from God because "…the wages of sin is death, but the gift of God is eternal life in Christ Jesus our Lord" (Romans 6:23). There are many who hope that the good things they have done throughout their life will outweigh the bad. However, the Bible tells us that "all our righteous acts are like filthy rags" (Isaiah 64:6b) and "There is no one righteous, not even one" (Romans 3:10b).

However, the good news is that God desires to have a personal and loving relationship with you. And He provides a way to make this possible. God loves you so much that "He gave His one and only Son, that whoever believes in Him shall not perish but have eternal life" (John 3:16b). Furthermore, "God demonstrates His own love for us in this: While we were still sinners, Christ died for us" (Romans 5:8). And we are told "that Christ died for our sins according to the Scriptures, that He was buried, that He was raised on the third day according to the Scriptures" (1 Corinthians 15:3b–4).

Jesus is the only one that can offer forgiveness and make a relationship with God possible. He said, "I am the way and the truth and the life. No one comes to the Father except through Me" (John 14:6b). In order to receive God's free gift to enter into a personal relationship with Him, there is a step that He invites us to take. This step is, "If you declare with your mouth, 'Jesus is Lord,' and believe in your heart that God raised Him from the dead, you will be saved. For it is with your heart that you believe and are justified, and it is with your mouth that you profess your faith and are saved" (Romans 10:9–10).

If you want to ask Jesus to come into your heart and life, I suggest the following words that you can repeat out loud (or in your heart) to Him. Or you could choose your own wording.

> *Dear Jesus,*
> *I confess that I am a sinner and have sinned against You. Please forgive me for all the wrong things that I have ever done toward You and others.*
> *I ask You to come into my heart and life. Please save me from the consequences of my sins, including eternal death. I believe that You died on the cross for my sins and rose from the dead to make a way for me to have eternal life. I choose to put my faith and trust in You, Jesus, by believing who You say You are according to the Bible: "I am the way and the truth*

and the life. No one comes to the Father except through Me" (John 14:6b).

Jesus, I ask You to be my Savior. I choose to make You Lord of my life. Please help me to walk in Your ways. Thank You, Jesus, for forgiving my sins and accepting me so that I can live with You in Your heavenly kingdom for all eternity, in Jesus' name.

Amen.

If you sincerely prayed this prayer, I welcome you as a new brother or sister in Christ and as a member of God's eternal family and heavenly kingdom. I suggest you take time to tell someone. It would be good to begin your new spiritual journey by reading the Book of John in the Bible. Also, it would be good to visit a Bible-believing fellowship of other Christians. You can commemorate this important day that you prayed this prayer, which is your spiritual birthday, by recording your name and the date that you prayed to accept Christ in the blanks provided below.

Name: _____

Date: _____

For "Everyone who believes that Jesus is the Christ is born of God" (1 John 5:1a). "For you have been born again... through the living and enduring word of God" (1 Peter 1:23a, c). "For the wages of sin is death, but the gift of God is eternal life in Christ Jesus our Lord" (Romans 6:23). I hope and pray that you have chosen to receive God's gift so that this eternal life will be in your future.

If you have prayed this prayer, please email me, David Hill, at thebarnbydavidhill@gmail.com.

AFTERWORD

Do You Desire Everything That Life Offers?

I f you accepted Jesus Christ as your Lord and Savior, you might consider asking yourself this question, "Do I desire every spiritual blessing and gift that God wants me to have?" If your answer is yes, then this invitation is for you.

Believers who have accepted Jesus as their personal Savior and Lord should expect and earnestly seek the baptism in the Holy Spirit. Jesus instructed His original twelve disciples in the New Testament, "Do not leave Jerusalem, but wait for the gift My Father promised, which you have heard Me speak about. For John baptized with water, but in a few days you will be baptized with the Holy Spirit" (Acts 1:4b–5). Peter, one of the twelve disciples of Jesus, told us,

Repent and be baptized, every one of you, in the name of Jesus Christ so that your sins may be forgiven. And you will receive the gift of the Holy Spirit [the baptism in the Holy Spirit]. The promise is for you

and your children and for all who are far off—for all
whom the Lord our God will call.

—Acts 2:38b–39

There are examples recorded in the Bible about how after Jesus' disciples received the baptism in the Holy Spirit, that it was their mission to ensure everyone else received this baptism.

When the apostles in Jerusalem heard that Samaria
had accepted the word of God [accepted Christ], they
sent Peter and John to them. When they arrived, they
prayed for the new believers there that they might
receive the Holy Spirit, because the Holy Spirit had
not yet come upon any of them; they had simply
been baptized in the name of the Lord Jesus. Then
Peter and John placed their hands on them, and they
received the Holy Spirit.

—Acts 8:14–17

A second example is also recorded in the Book of Acts.

And [the apostle Paul] asked them, "Did you receive
the Holy Spirit when you believed?" They answered,
"No, we have not even heard that there is a Holy
Spirit." So Paul asked, "Then what baptism did you
receive?" "John's baptism," they replied. Paul said,
"John's baptism was a baptism of repentance. He told
the people to believe in the one coming after him, that
is, Jesus." On hearing this, they were baptized into the

name of the Lord Jesus. When Paul placed his hands
on them, the Holy Spirit came on them, and they spoke
in tongues and prophesied.

—Acts 19:2–6

All believers need the baptism of the Holy Spirit because with it comes the enduement of power to be a witness for God overflowing with spiritual fullness. He also positions the believer to receive other supernatural gifts. Jesus said, "But you will receive power when the Holy Spirit comes on you; and you will be My witnesses in Jerusalem, and in all Judea and Samaria, and to the ends of the earth" (Acts 1:8). "And these signs will accompany those who believe: In My name they will drive out demons; they will speak in new tongues...they will place their hands on sick people, and they will get well" (Mark 16:17–18c). The apostle Paul wrote,

To one there is given through the Spirit [the Holy
Spirit] a message of wisdom, to another a message of
knowledge by means of the same Spirit, to another
faith by the same Spirit, to another gifts of healing
by that one Spirit, to another miraculous powers, to
another prophecy, to another the ability to distinguish
between spirits, to another the ability to speak in dif-
ferent kinds of tongues, and to still another the inter-
pretation of tongues. All these are the work of one and
the same Spirit, and He gives them to each one, just as
He determines.

— 1 Corinthians 12:8–11

As the previous Scripture passages indicate, the baptism in the Holy Spirit is a subsequent experience to salvation in Christ. However, there are biblical examples as well as modern-day testimonies that the baptism of the Holy Spirit can be received at the same time that one accepts Christ as Savior. This baptism can and has also been received in many cases, including mine, without having a full understanding of what the baptism in the Holy Spirit is. The evidence of receiving the baptism in the Holy Spirit is speaking in other tongues or a new language as the Holy Spirit enables. "All of them [Jesus' disciples] were filled with the Holy Spirit and began to speak in other tongues as the Spirit enabled them" (Acts 2:4).

I encourage you to ask God to baptize you in the Holy Spirit. There are numerous biblical accounts that support this powerful and life-changing experience, including those described in the Book of Acts. Simply tell Jesus with the sincerity of your heart that you desire to be baptized in the Holy Spirit. Ask Him to help you speak the new language that He has for you. As is necessary to receive Christ, receiving the baptism in the Holy Spirit requires that you also take another step of faith. You simply need to open your mouth and start speaking while believing that as you speak, the Holy Spirit's presence will enable you to release your tongue to speak in a new prayer language. "I would like every one of you to speak in tongues" (1 Corinthians 14:5a). "For anyone who speaks in a tongue does not speak to men but to God. Indeed, no one understands him; he utters mysteries with his spirit" (1 Corinthians 14:2).

In the last days, God says, I will pour out My Spirit on all people. Your sons and daughters will prophesy, your young men will see visions, your old men will dream dreams. Even on My servants, both men and women, I will pour out My Spirit in those days, and they will prophesy. And everyone who calls on the name of the Lord will be saved.

— Acts 2:17-18

Thankfully, I have received this wonderful and powerful gift; and I hope and pray that you will, too. If you have any questions, email me at thebarnbydavidhill@gmail.com.

Endnotes

1   Erma Durheim, *The Depression of The Dirty Thirties*,
    (Fairfield, Washington: Ye Galleon Press, 1992), page 16.

CPSIA information can be obtained
at www.ICGtesting.com
Printed in the USA
BVHW050713020223
657534BV00025B/458